In the Los Angeles ... elite secret spy u... Crime Intelligenc... of some targeted individuals keep expanding—even after their death ...

Division lore holds that OCID was perverted from the beginning—formed in the 1930s to scare off out-of-town gangsters and keep the rackets clear for home-town boys. Like the CIA, its goal was never to protect the public—it was to gather information. Under Chief Daryl Gates, the Division continued to operate in the tarnished tradition—and well outside the confines of the law:

- LAPD cops frequently played malicious pranks in minority neighborhoods, swooping down city blocks in faux assault modes, simply to enjoy the chaos of scattering residents. Other games included patrol cars boxing in and toying with baffled minority drivers.
- Reporters critical of the LAPD were targeted, put under surveillance, and harassed.
- False arrests were routine. A child-care counselor was falsely arrested for an alleged sex crime on the total whim of a vice cop. The couselor's career ended. The vice cop had no remorse.
- Cops spied on cops and other departments. Even within OCID's offices, cops bugged their colleagues and rifled their desks. The LAPD hierarchy even planted moles on the personal staff of the Police Commissioner.

IT ALL HAPPENED HERE, IN THE U.S.A. IT'S THE ULTIMATE CORRUPTION IN PUBLIC SERVICE ...

L.A. SECRET POLICE

Prologue

According to late-night comic lore, L.A. is supposed to be a dreamscape, a winterless fantasy of palmy sprawl where all the residents either subscribe to laughably phony gurus or genuflect to the creed of libertarian assault rifles and fluoride-free water. Whether they choose one path or the other, Los Angelenos are all, according to this interpretation, a zany collection of kooks. Not terribly astute, but often adorable, they are always entertaining. And if you keep an eye on them, you will know ahead of time just what waves of weirdness will transmit next over the Rockies. What a trip.

An entire regiment of comics made a good living exploiting this goofs-in-the-sunshine image, which has transmuted itself into a pop sociology wielding a mythological power of its own. The joke, perceived at first as only a joke, has gradually come to be accepted as a cute reality.

Meanwhile, over the years, a steady blue stream of Hollywood cop shows portrayed the City of Angels quite differently—as a nightmarish cauldron of ghoulish criminals. According to this script, the helpless potential victims of these omni-present urban brutes were spared awful deprada-tions only through the crisp, diligent work of the unappreciated, tough but fair, TV-handsome offi-cers of the Los Angeles Police Department, who always had hearts of gold.

The March 3, 1991, beating of black felon Rod-ney G. King by a group of white LAPD officers exploded the two conflicting myths. In the brutal scenario captured for 81 seconds by an amateur's video camera, several officers clubbed and kicked King over and over as he lay writhing on the ground. And a field sergeant, instead of stepping in to stop it, acted only to zap King with 50,000 volts from a laser. Also captured in the brutal footage shot by bystander George Holliday were irrepara-ble images of about twenty other cops standing around, doing nothing.

King was no choirboy. He was on parole for armed robbery. With two male passengers, he had been driving drunk after midnight. When police tried to pull him over, he turned off the freeway and sped through some red lights before he finally pulled over as several squad cars closed in. Then he got out of the car and did an impromptu dance, refusing to submit to handcuffs.

The first part of the videotape showed King, a husky young man, moving toward one of the officers. The last part showed his relentless beating and stomping. Among his injuries were a broken leg and a fractured cheekbone.

Critics had complained for years that LAPD cops meted out "street justice" to the poor, the nonwhite, the unconnected. The incidents, said these critics, were so widespread and so similar that they could not be viewed as isolated. This had to be policy. Look, said the critics, watch L.A.'s finest doing what they do best. This time it's on video-tape.

2

Now the criminals didn't look so formidable, the cops didn't act like Jack Webb or Martin Milner, and no one looked zany.

Chief Daryl F. Gates apologized for the beating. He called it an "aberration." Calls for his resignation intensified.

Cut to the afternoon of April 29, 1992. After more than a year of legal wrangling, the four officers indicted in the King beating were found not guilty. After seven days of deliberations, jurors were unable to reach a verdict on a single count of assault against Officer Laurence M. Powell, and Judge Stanley M. Weisberg declared a mistrial on that count. But the news that hit the street didn't delve into the small stuff. The cops got off. That's all anyone needed to hear.

Mayor Tom Bradley, a black ex-cop and civil libertarian, appealed for calm on television. But he vowed: "We will not accept renegade behavior by a few cops."

Minutes later, news helicopters buzzed like bees over the corner of Florence and Normandie in South Central Los Angeles. Down below, gangs of thugs were heaving rocks and bottles at passing vehicles and pulling out hapless nonblack drivers, beating them viciously. Many of the rioters were Crips, Bloods, and other gang grunts brittle and strung out from years of crack cocaine and endless street wars. They knew little about pity, less about remorse, lots about violence.

The immediacy and omnipresence of television were once again part of the story. But this time there was no videotape delay. The mayhem was being broadcast live, and everyone in L.A. seemed to know what was going on at Florence and Normandie except the police, who were nowhere to be seen. Where were the tough legions of the Marine-like Los Angeles Police Department?

The cops had been at the scene in force, then

ordered to retreat. A lieutenant from the 77th Street Station set up a command post and staging area at a nearby bus depot, and the station's patrol units were all ordered to proceed from there. But despite entreaties bordering on mutiny from his underlings, the lieutenant kept his cops at the command center—waiting for what, it wasn't clear. The reasons for this stalling and delay were disputed later as top cops took turns pointing fingers at each other. But in the postmortem, just about everybody agreed that much of the department was gripped by an inexplicable paralysis.

"The command post turned into a big black hole that sucked officers in and didn't spit them out," one sergeant later recalled.

The corner was abandoned to the whims of the mob for three horrible hours while police commanders sorted out their priorities. LAPD higher-ups shuttled in and out of the command post, grim-faced, barely speaking to the glaring grunts, who eagerly awaited orders.

In many ways the lean, mean LAPD modeled itself more after an elite army than a police force, and the tragedy playing itself out in South Central should have been right up its parade ground.

Gates, while still an LAPD comer, had been credited with developing the very first Special Weapons and Tactics team (SWAT) formed in the United States. SWAT tactics were clearly modeled after those of an infantry platoon. Now that this famed police tactician was chief of the department, where were the tactics? Where were the cops when you needed them? Field commanders later admitted that there had been no contingency plans to deal with the disturbances. Everyone awaited a superstrategy from the top, which, if it existed, never reached the field.

And as it turned out, when the rioting began, most of the field captains were attending a seminar in Oxnard, about 40 miles north of the city. Back in Los Angeles, the afternoon shift was coming on duty. Day-shift cops, generally more streetwise than their superiors, asked if they should stay on the job. In most instances they were told no, there's no authorization.

As word of the rioting spread, Chief Gates spit in the eye of fate. He left his office at Parker Center headquarters to attend a political fund-raiser in upper-crust Brentwood. The gathering had been organized to fight Proposition F, a ballot measure that dared to amend the city charter to make the chief more accountable to elected officials. On his way out, a reporter asked Gates about the police response at Florence and Normandie. Gates, authoritative and brusque, said his officers would handle it.

Police Commission President Stanley K. Sheinbaum, former chairman of the American Civil Liberties Union of Southern California, pulled into the parking lot behind Parker Center as Gates was getting into his car. Gates and Sheinbaum were on about the same terms as Harry Truman and Douglas MacArthur just before the president fired his general. "I asked him where he was going," Sheinbaum recalled later, but the chief didn't stop. "He said he had something to do."

Rioting spread like cancer. Reports of looting and arson tumbled in from new locations. Armed men were waylaying public buses, marching off the passengers, then beating and robbing them. In area hospitals, even children were turning up as casualties. Cops in the lower echelons asked permission to go in and at least rescue the motorists at Florence and Normandie, where each moment of violent TV imagery dug a deeper pit for the LAPD. Wait for orders, they were told.

A few cops, against orders, tried to get there on their own, but sniper fire was heavy, and the streets were clogged with rioters and abandoned cars. The cops were beaten back. Its leadership in confusion, the LAPD was an organization that appeared to be upside-down and torpid, like a half-dead turtle. And the city in its care crumbled under the rage of a mob.

Cops who were on the street every day knew how this would play out in the news media: Los Angeles police officers were excessively brutal when they had helpless suspect King on the ground and inexcusably timid while gangs of felons brutalized innocents in the South Central spine of the city.

At 6:46 P.M., more than three hours after the verdicts were delivered, white trucker Reginald O. Denny arrived, unaware, at the intersection of Florence and Normandie. He was yanked out of his truck like a flour sack. The terrible assault on him that followed was the worst yet, searing itself, blow by blow, kick by kick, into the memories of all who witnessed it. And hundreds of thousands did see it on live TV, as exuberant thugs assaulted Denny with fists, bricks, even the fire extinguisher he carried in his truck.

Most views of the assault were shot from the helicopters overhead. The topside camera angles added to the lunacy of it all, turning viewers into unwilling spectators, hypnotized above the tortures at the Roman Colosseum. It was impossible to watch and impossible to turn away. At one point an assailant, after smashing Denny with a brick, stopped to do a little dance. There seemed to be a competition going on. What can we do to him next? They crushed his face like an aluminum can.

Now Los Angelenos of all races cried for their city and for the two symbols of their despair— Rodney King and Reginald Denny.

Two of the four black citizens who would eventually rescue Denny and get him to Daniel Freeman Memorial Hospital learned of his plight from television. Everyone else just assumed someone in an official capacity would get to him and administer aid; no one did. The four samaritans were two men and two women—a laid-off data control technician, an out-of-work aerospace engineer, a nutritionist, and a young man in black who was never identified.

The first rescuers reached Denny about twenty minutes after his attackers, evidently bored, moved on to other pursuits. He had somehow managed to get back behind the wheel, but his eyes were swollen shut, his face covered in blood. He was trying to drive through the hostile shouting, the chaos, and burning cars, but his getaway was proceeding an inch at a time.

The engineer and the data technician tried to clear a path with their car while the nutritionist stayed in the truck cab with Denny. Then the young man in black showed up. The others feared he was a gang member come to finish Denny off. Instead, he slid behind the wheel and drove the big rig to the hospital as the nutritionist peered around the shattered windshield and shouted directions. When the emergency room crew grabbed Denny, now in convulsions, the young man delivered the truck back to Denny's employer, hopped out, and disappeared.

Weeks later, LAPD detectives, using videotapes as their evidence, identified suspects in the Denny beating. A force the size of a full infantry company —200 officers—swarmed into the neighborhood during the early morning hours to nab one of the suspects. They went in as if they were storming Omaha Beach, taking the high ground, clearing the area, everybody covering everybody else with massive firepower. When the suspect was safely in hand, Chief Gates, escorted by TV cameras, personally went in and made the arrest.

Lt. Mike Moulin was the ill-fated supervisor who had ordered his officers to retreat from Florence and Normandie and later directed the bus depot command post. Said Moulin: "If I had two hundred officers for every one suspect on the street, I never would have had to pull out."

On March 19, 1992, a year after the King beating, five weeks before one of the most savage riots in United States history, the police commission was in the final stages of a search for a new police chief. Commission President Sheinbaum, Commissioner Anne Reiss Lane, and former Commissioner Reva Tooley pulled into the parking lot of a shopping center in Cerritos, a blue-collar suburb of Los Angeles, where they met a former LAPD detective named Mike Rothmiller.

Sheinbaum had sought the meeting, which was arranged by Ramona Ripston, director of the Los Angeles chapter of the ACLU.

Rothmiller had left the department in 1983 after being seriously injured in a mysterious attempt on his life. He had been working in a little-known LAPD outpost called the Organized Crime Intelligence Division. No one knew very much about OCID except the fifty-seven detectives who worked there. It received almost no press attention, and those who did know of the unit's existence just assumed the name told the story, that OCID pursued mobsters.

But over the years, some of the police commissioners grew to suspect there was more to OCID than could be discerned by the name on its door. They believed there might be a link between the workings of OCID and the department's intimate knowledge of what was going on among politicians and other big players around Southern California, people with no ties to any crime, organized or not.

All too often, the chief and his cohorts seemed to know what was going to happen before it happened. And when the commissioners inquired about just what OCID was up to, they got standard, textbook answers.

After rendezvousing in the parking lot, Tooley, the two commissioners, and Rothmiller went to the nearby Hoff's Hut restaurant, where Rothmiller answered questions for two and a half hours.

What Rothmiller confirmed, in essence, was that for years the LAPD had tricked its critics into watching the birdie. The birdie was the Political Disorder Intelligence Division, long rumored to be the center of LAPD intrigues directed against its perceived enemies within the L.A. establishment.

And in fact, the PDID was far from pure. Over the years it had spied on a host of organizations that included the PTA and World Council of Churches. In 1983, years after the police commission had ordered the PDID to destroy more than 50,000 espionage files, many of them turned up in the home of a cop.

In response, the commission then ordered the PDID to disband entirely. It did, and reemerged with a new name, the Anti-Terrorist Division. But Rothmiller confirmed the commissioner's suspicions that the dirtiest of the LAPD's dirty work had been done all along neither by the PDID or its mutated Anti-Terrorist Division successor. It was OCID they should have been watching.

For OCID, unbeknownst to both friends and enemies of the LAPD, maintained secret, Stalinesque dossiers, some of them kept in privately rented storage units; there were files on virtually every mover and shaker in Southern California.

The ultrasensitive information in the files was assembled by detectives in OCID and then turned over to a captain. Unlike other captains in the department, this one had no buffers between himself and the top. He reported directly to Big Brother: Chief Daryl F. Gates, himself the former OCID captain.

Rothmiller also confirmed that among the detectives on the OCID roster were two men assigned exclusively to political espionage—the political team. Sometimes assisted by other OCID detectives, sometimes not, these two supertrusted beings usually conducted the most sensitive operations. And they didn't report to the captain who reported to the chief. They reported directly to the chief.

At Rothmiller's Hoff Hut meeting, the commissioners said they suspected there were bugs and taps in place at their homes and offices. Rothmiller, always precise in these matters, told them he could not confirm their suspicions. He could only confirm that OCID had undertaken such operations in the past and had the equipment and know-how to undertake them now. The commissioners, he said, should just assume their conversations were overheard. The commissioners told Rothmiller they had long ago made that assumption.

The commissioners also told Rothmiller they suspected there were two moles planted on their staff who were direct pipelines to the chief. Could Rothmiller verify this? He concluded that from his experience as a detective in Gates's OCID, he would be very much surprised if there were only two such moles. LAPD officers on the commission staff were assigned by the LAPD hierarchy. They were lifers. They were there before the commissioners and would remain there after the commissioners were gone. Essentially, the LAPD foxes were expected to guard the chicken coop.

During his five years inside OCID, Rothmiller had never personally debriefed moles on the commission staff. But he had seen written reports detailing political team debriefings of the LAPD mole on Mayor Bradley's staff—Bradley's driver.

The officials made clear that they assumed OCID practices hadn't changed since Rothmiller left the department. But they wanted to know what he knew about it. Rothmiller, who, since leaving the department had been assisting ACLU's Ramona Ripston in her attempts to make the unit conform to the law, explained that he maintained good sources within the unit. Yes, he said, it was all still going on. Technology had changed, along with some of the personnel, but the essential characteristics of the secret police unit were the same.

The officials questioning Rothmiller were surprised at none of this. They showed concern, but they also showed relief, the kind of relief people display when their fears are confronted and then confirmed. Now they had a map of where to look, and they could plan their next moves with more assurance.

The list of candidates to succeed Chief Gates contained the name of only one individual outside the LAPD, Commissioner Willie L. Williams of the Philadelphia Police Department. Sheinbaum asked Rothmiller if it was possible for any of the other candidates, all of them assistant chiefs and deputy chiefs, to be ignorant of the abuses perpetrated by the OCID detectives for the chief.

"I don't think so," said Rothmiller.

Would Rothmiller brief the new chief so he could get a road map to the abuse and dirty tricks? Yes, Rothmiller told Sheinbaum, providing the new chief came from outside the department.

Don't worry, Sheinbaum replied, he will.

Rothmiller's story, the beating of Rodney King, the South Central eruption, and the tepid LAPD response remain very much connected. Because

Rothmiller attested to a police department hierarchy so obsessed with power, so inured to its own misuse of that power, that it no longer understood or pursued its mission. And that's where the LAPD was that April day the city began to burn.

Pursuing other priorities.

· 1 ·

Stealth

It was a warm August night in 1982, just about midnight. A helmeted figure on a motorcycle tore out of the darkness, pulled alongside an unmarked LAPD car moving down a residential street in suburban Orange County, and emptied a machine pistol at the cop inside, Detective Mike Rothmiller.

Rothmiller, who spotted trouble moments before the barrage, braked hard and snapped the wheel to the right, barreling his vehicle down a five-foot embankment. He heard the pop, pop, pop of the weapon, saw the muzzle flash.

Behind the wheel, he felt like a naked target strapped inside a rolling casket. He had to bail out. The car still moving, he tumbled out the door and hit the ground hard. The wind sailed out of his chest. Later, looking back through the mist of split-second terror and confusion, he remembers trying to crawl back to the car to reach the radio and get help—an irrational move. No LAPD radios would work in this gully. But he was fumbling for the mike. And there was a voice calling from somewhere that asked him, "Are you okay?

13

Are you okay?" He reached for the .38 revolver strapped to his ankle, but the voice was friendly. "Are you okay? Are you okay?"

Bleeding from the right side of his chest, dazed, a numbing sensation in his lower legs, an excruciating pain in his lower back, Rothmiller almost laughed in reply to the disembodied voice. But no laugh came. No, he thought, he wasn't feeling terribly okay. He found out later the question came from an off-duty fireman who lived nearby. As for the button man, he'd already taken off.

The fireman spoke to Rothmiller. Rothmiller doesn't remember what was said. Did he hear it? He remembered a soothing voice, then other voices. And sirens. A helicopter hovered overhead, shining a terrible light, drowning confusion into worse confusion. There was no help for his pain. He just lay there. Shouldn't somebody be doing something? Then a cop leaned over him. Rothmiller grabbed the cop by his Sam Brown belt. "Go check on my wife," he screamed over the helicopter noise. "Right away. The guy followed me from my house." He gave the address and a description of the assassin. There wasn't much. A fast bike, dark clothing, full-shaded helmet.

By the time paramedics arrived, Rothmiller could no longer feel the right side of his body. They put him in a neck brace, hooked him up to an I.V., and rushed him in an ambulance to Fountain Valley Regional Trauma Center. But Rothmiller didn't feel like he was rushing anywhere. Everything moved in agonizing slow motion, even though the ambulance was bouncing, flying over the bumps, speeding. Speeding but getting nowhere.

"He's been shot," a paramedic said, looking at the wound in his side.

Somebody measured his blood pressure. "Faster," a paramedic yelled. "We're losing this guy."

14

He thought, "Damn, I'm going to die. But I'm breathing okay now." He couldn't understand: you shouldn't die when you're breathing. But he believed the paramedics and with each breath he expected to die.

At the hospital's trauma center, the medical team cut off his clothes and went to work. They stuck a catheter in him. "This is going to hurt," a doctor said afterward. How could anything hurt more? Rothmiller wondered, though not for long. They punctured him below the navel and filled his abdominal cavity with a saline solution, then pressed down on his chest, draining him with the catheter. He was being crushed. Each breath was a gasp for life.

But results were good. No internal bleeding. They took X rays. "Here's some good news," a doctor told the externally bleeding Rothmiller. "You weren't shot after all." The blood oozing from his side came from a laceration. But after a CAT scan, the doctors determined that his spinal column had been bruised.

Wheeled out in the hallway, he found his wife, Nancy. She was safe. She was crying, but she spoke to him firmly and kissed him. "It'll be okay," she said. And he was starting to believe maybe it would be okay.

His police lieutenant showed up for a visit. "Listen, whatever you do," the lieutenant said, "don't tell Huntington Beach too much, okay? They're going to interview you." He meant Huntington Beach Police Department investigators. The shooting was on their turf. "You can talk to them some, but don't tell them about your cases, understand? Don't tell them too much." And when his LAPD captain came, he wasn't to say anything about the car.

"What?"

"Don't tell him anything about the car," the lieutenant repeated. Rothmiller unsuccessfully tried to shape the meaning of this in his mind. In his unit, the detectives all took city cars home, but if they lived outside the county, as Rothmiller did, technically, they were supposed to park them somewhere on government property, such as at a power station. But of course no one did. The lieutenant took his car home too. And he lived in Orange County as well.

Somebody had just tried to murder Rothmiller and the lieutenant was worried about parking. And advising him not to say too much to the investigators. Keep everything secret—but Rothmiller was used to all this. It wasn't just a bad dream. Secrets were what he dealt in, all right. He and the lieutenant and everyone else in his unit. They found them out and they kept them. They had to keep the secrets.

When the Huntington Beach detective interviewed him minutes later, Rothmiller did what he was told. He spoke about the shooting, but not the cases he was working on.

"They were asking him the same questions over and over," remembers Nancy Rothmiller, "and he was clearly in shock. He was shaking. I knew I couldn't make them stop. I started to pass out. A nurse gave me smelling salts."

Then the lieutenant came back. "I just called Hamilton," he said. "Somebody tried to get in his house tonight." Rothmiller's partner, Ken Hamilton, lived a few blocks from Rothmiller, near the scene of the shooting.

The Hamiltons called patrol officers, but they didn't snare anyone.

Rothmiller was wired like a rock guitar. The trauma of it all sank deeper, and the shrieking pain mixed curiously with numbness down his leg. He was in a room somewhere. A nurse gave him a shot.

16

He felt just as bad. Confused, worried for everything. The nurse returned and gave him another shot. This one brought troubled sleep.

Back at the crash site, detectives from the LAPD and Huntington Beach Police Department found several slugs lodged in Rothmiller's vehicle. Piecing together events, they were puzzled by the would-be killer's method. They'd never seen a hit man work this way. This was before assassins around the world made the motorcycle hit a kind of precision signature for sleek, sudden death. It caught on because it allowed the shooter to get close to his prey, kill him, and then get away, all in a flash.

The preferred weapon, as it was this night, was a .22-caliber semiautomatic pistol, probably a Ruger, specially rigged to fire an automatic burst of long-rifle slugs. Easily concealed, easily disposed of, deadly fast. Faster than most people are likely to think or see.

The next day, Rothmiller was placed in the intensive care unit registered under a phony name. LAPD officers began an around-the-clock watch.

Also that day, four men were observed pulling up to the bank where Rothmiller's wife, Nancy, was a bank officer. They watched the building for a while, one with binoculars. It was another warm August day in Southern California, yet one of these men wore a trench coat. They watched the spot where Nancy Rothmiller would normally sit, next to a glass exterior wall. But she wasn't there, and they took off. The bank manager called the police. The LAPD had already told Nancy the night of the shooting not to go to work for a while.

Both numb and in pain, Rothmiller arrived home a few days later, escorted by LAPD cops. At the house, he was greeted by an LAPD SWAT team, which guarded him and Nancy day and night for the next several weeks. It was Mike, Nancy, and five to seven cops, all staying at their three-bedroom house. The phone was always ringing. Cops were always on watch, so the TV never went off. Life refused to go back to the way it was. Mike's pain wouldn't go away.

Another SWAT team was placed at his partner Hamilton's residence.

The attempted murder and events surrounding it might have been one of the biggest L.A. stories of the year. But nothing was entered on the police blotter, and nothing appeared in the news media. The incident was treated like one of the old Stalinist nonevents of the thirties or forties—an ignored plane crash or a flood on the steppes—a tree falling in a silent forest. The ability to smother the story was a display of splendid stealth and crushing power—the stealth and power of LAPD's Organized Crime Intelligence Division (OCID).

Rothmiller didn't know it yet, but a chapter in his life was ending. A cop for ten years at the time, he would leave the force sixteen months later. It wasn't what he wanted.

Since 1978, he had been an investigator within the enigmatic OCID, a unit that didn't confine its investigations to organized criminals, despite its name.

The OCID sleuths operated out of the third floor of a windowless, low-profile structure across from the Greyhound bus station along the edge of downtown. The cops called the place Fort Davis, in homage to ex-Chief Ed Davis, who clearly had the building designed to withstand a military siege.

The OCID offices were so festooned with electronic bugs and taps, they could have passed a KGB inspection. From these rooms the unit's detectives quietly and painstakingly gathered intelligence on enormous lists of people who may or may not have been suspected of wrongdoing.

OCID's captain reported directly to L.A.'s chief of police about who was straight and who was gay, who was left and who was right, who was friend and who was foe. And once someone's name found its way into OCID files, that file would never be extracted.

OCID moved around, duplicated, triplicated, and sometimes even shredded its files. But they always turned up later, like Houdini's rabbits or Kilroy cartoons. And the most sensitive files were secreted away in untraceable public storage units, out of reach of ACLU pests or silly court orders.

Meanwhile, each fact, each rumor, each supposition became currency, a negotiable instrument that might be traded or used to find more rumors or facts, all in a quest to enhance the power of the LAPD hierarchy. When the chief craved dirt on a potential rival or wished to get the lowdown on his daughter's future in-laws, it was OCID that did the dirty work.

During the furor over the King beating, the public across the nation began to question the caliber of Chief Daryl Gates's leadership. But Gates, with unshakable support from a majority of city council members, somehow maneuvered through the storm of outrage for more than a year, clinging to his post like a barnacle on steroids. When Mayor Bradley asked Gates to resign, he simply refused. Then, when the police commission placed Gates on a sixty-day leave, the city council stepped in the next day and reinstated him.

Gates wielded power in Los Angeles in much the same way J. Edgar Hoover once ruled Washington. In place like a rock, he seemed to possess some mysterious key to personal survival. But the key was no mystery to anyone in OCID.

After all, its agents spent countless man-hours stalking city council members in preparation for just such an emergency. Because of OCID, the LAPD had secret files on the gay council member hiding in the closet and on the council member who was sleeping with an aide. The department had intelligence files on questionable deals and campaign funding and a mountain of other embarrassing, sticky business. As soon as someone declared candidacy, a full-scale investigation began. OCID had files on everything and everybody who counted.

This ultrasecret political espionage was coordinated by two detectives on the Sphinx-like political team. When the political team conducted political espionage that could not be handled by only two investigators, they assembled larger teams composed of themselves and other OCID detectives. These teams were dubbed quiet teams.

Only the brass above OCID and the detectives within ever heard the words *quiet team*. They were code. Anyone who used them was in on the secret. Quiet teams did the political dirty work that police critics speculated was being done somewhere within in the bowels of the LAPD. No one knew precisely who was doing it. Quiet teams were very quiet.

OCID chose its recruits carefully. It assembled a palace guard of experts in every field of investigation that counted—from illegal electronic surveillance to undercover work, from deductive reasoning skills to street-fighting prowess. There were interrogation masters, rubber-hose artists, and lock men. OCID had a wide net of informants and money to pay them. Its formidable assets were all put to work to gather the information that ended up in OCID's files.

There were many ways a name could end up in OCID files, but the surest ticket into a file drawer was the City of Angels' sleekest, best-known product—fame. OCID actually devoted much of its energy into putting out a kind of private *People* magazine for the chief's office.

Using an elaborate intelligence network of informants and bugs, surveillances and devices to intercept phone calls, OCID operatives monitored all kinds of celebrities—politicians, union leaders, Hollywood stars, professional athletes, team owners, TV and print journalists.

Muhammad Ali, Connie Chung, Alan Cranston, Rock Hudson, Sam Yorty, Sugar Ray Leonard, Sandy Koufax, Robert Redford, Tommy Lasorda, and assorted church prelates were all fair game. Celebrities didn't have to be suspected of anything specific because after all, everyone was suspect. Everyone had a skeleton in the closet somewhere.

Political "enemies" like Ramona Ripston of the ACLU were targeted along with "friends" like columnist Pat Buchanan and utterly nonpolitical entities such as Michael Jackson.

This raw information on newsworthy figures became an end in itself as real police work was shunted aside in the eternal search for juicier gossip. OCID operatives routinely debriefed the mole on the mayor's staff, wrote down what Sinatra ordered for lunch, tailed congressmen, and investigated various malicious rumors.

All of which was enough to make a good cop laugh. Or cry. And there were still some good cops in OCID. But of all the requirements set down for would-be entrants to this elite unit, secrecy was paramount. These were cops who knew how to keep their mouths shut. By the time entering detectives discovered the essence of their mission, they were already trapped inside an iron wall of *omertà* as imposing as any erected by the Sicilian mob.

Meanwhile, life inside the unit was relatively sweet. All the detectives had expense accounts, just like the executives in those glass towers along Wilshire Boulevard. Accounting procedures were loose as old sweatsocks. In some ways OCID cadres actually lived the roles of movie detectives; life imitated art. No roll calls, the investigators drove city cars home, and they were officially on the job whenever they called in and said so. They could choose their own cases and how to work them.

If they were short of something to do, they could volunteer to work surveillance on someone else's case or make out reports based on rumors. Rumors were always welcome at OCID.

And who wouldn't want to be privy to all that raw data on the rich and famous? OCID remained the ultimate goal for good LAPD detectives. And once they got inside, even though the reality might not live up to their expectations, they weren't about to go back to chasing stinkbugs around little corners of L.A. As cops, they had all seen enough of life to understand that the view from the top rarely equaled the anticipation of the climb. It was unheard of for anyone to seek a transfer.

After a while, because they weren't required to solve crimes or seek prosecutions, most of OCID agents fell into a lazy, slow-motion pattern that was more in keeping with the movie-set facade of laid-back California than the grimmer reality of L.A.'s tough streets. But some of them took the name of their unit seriously; they made cases against gangsters.

Ironically, they did so not because they were OCID detectives but in spite of it. Because the unit's leaders were so hungry for dirt, they forgot or ignored the original purpose for having police. OCID's goal was not to protect the public; it was information. Undercover OCID detectives who actually spent their time investigating mobsters routinely observed dope buys and concealed weapons and all manner of felonies they were instructed to ignore.

This made them less like cops and more like CIA or KGB agents. Their function was to bring back data and let their bosses decide what, if anything, should be done with it. Arrests could jeopardize the flow. "We have to look at the big picture," commanders would say. And OCID personnel would then have to trust that there was indeed a big picture, somewhere.

Meanwhile, a new OCID detective quickly learned that busts brought instant heat from above. His least-used piece of equipment became his handcuffs.

The LAPD brass knew from the start that it was absolutely imperative to shed as little light as possible on OCID. And since its formation in 1957, the division had barely been noticed by the news media. Los Angeles was a city swarming with reporters, but most of them worked for just one newspaper, the *Los Angeles Times*. So there was essentially just one city desk to fool. And the TV journalists were, for the most part, completely unaware of what was going on.

So L.A. journalists never seemed to ask just what detectives in the Organized Crime Intelligence Division did for a living. If OCID made arrests, that could change. There would be publicity. But even worse than reporters were the lawyers who attracted reporters. If there were arrests, attorneys for the people arrested might try to subpoena files or put detectives on the stand and ask them what they were up to: "How did you happen to get hold of this piece of information?" Such questions wouldn't do. The bottom line remained: no arrests.

OCID cops who wanted to behave like cops had to do it under the table, just like the criminals they pursued. A favorite ploy was to conspire with other police agencies. The detectives would wait until their prey planned a crime, say, in Orange County or Nevada or New York or Chicago, and then tip off police there. It wasn't as satisfying, but it had to do.

Other times, because the information had to go to another LAPD division, frustrated OCID detectives were reduced to anonymously calling a privately funded 1–800 crime-tip line that relayed their tip from the national center back to the appropriate LAPD division. It was like having to go around the world to get back to where they ought to be in the first place.

But OCID detectives were used to both shortcuts and the long way around. And they were used to dealing with cops outside the LAPD. Especially other intelligence cops. Units resembling OCID could be found all over the world. They even formed their own association, Law Enforcement Intelligence Units. A regularly updated membership directory listed in-house phone numbers and contacts within each of approximately 300 member agencies, allowing operatives to network like yuppies, only on an international basis.

If a case did have international ties, OCID could sometimes profit from even looser controls over police methods elsewhere. For example, if a case reached to Mexico, friendly federales were not averse to beating information out of suspects for OCID. If it had Canadian ties, the Royal Canadian Police could place a tap on any phone they wished without court approval or sliding under the law.

When his would-be assassin sprang out of the night, Rothmiller had been working on two international cases involving a form of underworld trade that these days has become practically routine—drugs in, guns out.

He just hadn't been much interested in reporting what movie stars ate for lunch.

Rothmiller has the kind of voice you might hear from a TV correspondent. It's user-friendly, a deep voice that's authoritative without being authoritarian. And like a network correspondent, he gets to the point politely and fast.

He grew up in the working-class area of South Gate, in the white-smoke industrial belt stretching north from the harbor at San Pedro into an arc around the eastern edges of Los Angeles. It was several hundred sociological light-years from the West Side boutiques, bistros, and Spanish mansions that tourists see—a neighborhood that produced cops, defense workers, an occasional scientist or accountant, an occasional street criminal.

In high school, he was a sturdy kid who grew to a shade under six feet, a crafty right-handed pitcher who also played the outfield because he could hit the ball. An untroubled kid looking for some kind of challenge, he learned to scuba dive and climb mountains.

After enrolling in community college, Rothmiller tried to join the fire department, but the white-male waiting list was two years long. Meanwhile, he enrolled in a special LAPD internship program that helped pay his college expenses.

At age twenty-one, the LAPD gave him a choice between entering the academy then or exiting the program, which would leave him unable to afford school anyway. "I was drafted into the LAPD," he would explain later with a smile and a shrug. He became an LAPD cadet, promising himself he would continue his studies later, even if he had to do it part-time. He kept his promise, earning a B.A. from the University of Redlands while on the force.

Rothmiller was accepted easily by other cops, but he was never a typical cop. He didn't have to be talking with a criminal or another cop to be comfortable with the conversation.

By concentrating his will, Rothmiller had managed to escape the soul-killing cynicism that tears down the lives of big-city cops. And year after year on OCID, he'd worked to distance himself from the division's tawdry espionage missions and do what he set out to do—solve crimes. He discovered that if he could fill up his time chasing real criminals, someone else could be found to tail Dean Martin's girlfriend. And so he buried himself in the work of a detective.

Rothmiller had been to enough cop funerals to know police weren't always as mournful of their dead as they liked to pretend. But there really was a code, an esprit de corps that demanded they at least stand together against any assailant.

Try to kill a cop and the department will jump in with both feet. That's what Rothmiller thought, lying low in his SWAT-guarded home. Hushing up everything, keeping it all out of the papers, didn't worry him. It was just a standard OCID reflex. Besides, he was still an LAPD cop, not some nameless intelligence agent felled in a Viennese alley.

The day following the shooting, his lieutenant had returned to the Intensive Care Unit for another visit. He told Rothmiller, "We have information there's a payoff on this deal." Someone had gotten to the Huntington Beach investigator, he said. "Remember, don't tell them too much. We'll take care of this. Don't worry. We'll take care of it in our own way."

And Rothmiller had no reason to disbelieve the lieutenant. But everything hurt, and he was uneasy about this, uneasy about waiting, about everything. He hung on to those words: "We'll take care of this." There were some awfully good detectives in OCID. Whatever needed to be done, they knew how to do it. Looked at in the proper light, the .22-caliber message from the midnight motorcycle geek was nothing less than a terrific clue, a master key to one of the open-case puzzles that both tantalized and fulfilled Rothmiller as a detective.

· 2 ·

Rules of the Game

T he dirty tricks and abusive methods employed by OCID were not unique to that elite division. They just happened to be exceptionally fine-tuned there. Everything done by the intelligence detectives was, in fact, grounded in standard LAPD procedure. The OCID detectives were merely the plainclothed shock troops of a department that had been out of control for some time. Ironically, being out of control was a tactic the department used to maintain control.

Rothmiller found this out his first week inside a patrol car. Fresh out of the academy, twenty-one years old, he was working out of the Wilshire division, eager to learn and of course frightened. His training officer: a taciturn white LAPD veteran.

After midnight, about an hour into their shift, the training officer pulled into the deserted parking lot of the Sears store on Pico. After a while another veteran officer pulled up in another patrol car and the two senior cops got out, motioning Rothmiller to do the same.

His two superiors both crossed their arms and looked hard at Rothmiller. He knew he was about to be tested.

"What did you think of the academy?" his training officer finally asked him.

An open-ended question. Rothmiller had no clue as to what they were looking for. He said the academy was not terribly difficult, although some of the physical training was tough.

"What do you think of working the Wilshire division?"

Rothmiller explained that he considered it an interesting piece of Los Angeles turf because its boundaries ranged from the tough slums of Baldwin Hills north across the Santa Monica Freeway into middle-class Fairfax and the wealthier areas of the West Side. It was a division with all kinds of people in it—blacks, Hispanics, lots of other ethnic groups. It must be a good place to patrol.

So far, so good, he thought.

"What do you think about niggers?" his training officer said, absolutely deadpan.

The rookie felt beads of sweat soaking into the fabric of his brand-new, freshly pressed wool uniform. He saw where this was headed, knew there was absolutely nothing he could do about it. Not in the real world.

Rothmiller had already finished two years of college. Like so many blue-collar kids trying to better his station in life, he wanted to stay clear of the ignorance and cruelty of racist attitudes. But that didn't seem to be what these two veterans had in mind.

Rothmiller mumbled something about how there were all kinds of people within different races, some of them good, some of them not so good.

"No," said the training officer, suddenly animated. "If you want to last here, if you want to survive, if you want to make probation, all niggers are fucked. Don't ever forget that."

Welcome to the Los Angeles Police Department, the rookie thought.

Standing there in the darkness, Rothmiller affected the same blank expression adopted by cops everywhere. This was something police officers learn early—to mask their true thoughts. And he wondered how any officer of the law could hope to befriend and protect citizens if he hated the citizens on sight.

At the time, he could only hope these two cops were rotten apples, exceptions to the rule. As the years went by he often thought about his indoctrination in the dark quiet of that parking lot. But by then he understood that those two men were not rotten exceptions at all.

They were typical LAPD cops. Racism was expected, part of the group persona. Shrink from it and you were an odd duck, perhaps a pink one. If someone didn't like it, the best he could do was refrain from contributing to the steady stream of race-tinged patter.

As it turned out, both of those experienced officers who informed Rothmiller of their dirty racist secret were, aside from that one faulty chromosome, nice guys. Rothmiller didn't particularly want to admit that to himself.

He wasn't the first individual to notice that racists don't always fit one brutal stereotype. They could be quite caring, personable people, with a terrible defect in their makeup. Clearly the gruesome mechanism that fired the racist psyche could be vastly complex. People didn't come in set packages. Their traits overlapped and contradicted one another.

And certainly not everyone on the LAPD shared the same faulty chromosome. But race hatred was nonetheless a dominating force.

Minority officers, especially blacks, were always on the outside, perpetual minor leaguers never quite admitted into the big leagues of LAPD acceptance. Most of them tried, some by being tougher on minorities than their white co-officers. Quick with an insult or a baton to the rib cage.

Blacks on the street also learned it was a mistake to call a black officer "Brother."

Rothmiller had spent his first night on the force with a black training officer, a soft-spoken, patient, streetwise cop. At the end of the shift, just as they were saying good-bye, the veteran told his charge: "Most of what you learned in the academy doesn't apply out here."

But Rothmiller already knew that. Because even in the academy, cadets already were being taught that there was an academy way and a real way.

Also, throughout their six months as cadets, Rothmiller and his classmates were warned over and over that they would be tested physically out on the street. They must show an eagerness to thump the enemy immediately or they wouldn't even make it to graduation.

"Never hit someone with a closed fist when you hit the street," their instructor said. "But if you do, go for the belly, the groin, or the kidney. You don't want to leave marks."

That was a common academy theme: Don't do it this way because it's against the rules. Then there would be a wink and an explanation of what was really expected.

During baton training, the instructor had spoken in flat tones, like a humanoid manual: "Target areas should be the upper torso or stomach. The shins provide target zones which produce severe pain without risking serious injury. Similarly the wrists are obvious targets since blows here will open the hand and most likely disable the subject. The idea is not to inflict corporal punishment."

Then he changed tone. Actually, he said, you hit the asshole anywhere you can. And don't get too close because that could result in a wrestling match. Stand back and swing for the fences.

Which is exactly what shocked viewers would see on the Rodney King videotape—LAPD officers doing what they were trained to do. This plain truth was at the core of the defense mounted by the officers charged with beating him.

Cadets were even told how to lie in order to neatly explain an infraction. "Never hit the guy in the head," Rothmiller's instructor said. "But if you do, you simply say the suspect ducked or moved. Always say you were going for the shoulder or the clavicle. You couldn't help it if the subject moved."

Also as a cadet, Rothmiller learned that he would be expected to falsify reports in order to make an arrest stick. This was all part of what department strategists called proactive policing. Proactive patrol, the LAPD crowed to its admirers, was how it managed to keep the city in line with a relatively small force.

If you don't like someone's looks, pull him over and see what's under his fingernails, an academy trainer told the eager cadets. You can always find P.C. (probable cause) later.

"Follow anyone for a block and he's sure to commit an infraction," the instructor said. "But even if he doesn't, you can always say he crossed over a double yellow line, he was following too close, something like that. Don't say it was an equipment violation, because then you would need physical evidence, such as a broken taillight."

An instructor also admonished them that lying on the witness stand could be grounds for perjury, but if a cop remembered something that might not help his case and then in his testimony he conveniently forgot it, he would be legally in the clear. "I don't recall" was recommended as a handy courtroom phrase. Such messages were not lost on the cadets. And they were quickly reinforced by their trainers when they made it to the street.

Later on as a probationer, Rothmiller and his training partner for the night were called to settle a dispute. Someone had thrown a flower pot through a plate-glass window. The resident stood on the second-floor terrace of her apartment and screamed out her story, pointing to a man down below standing with a crowd of neighbors.

"That motherfucker broke my window!" she raged.

Rothmiller's less than diplomatic partner pointed at the man: "Is that the nigger over there?"

"Yeah."

"Did you break the window?" asked the training officer.

"No, the bitch is lying!"

"All right, come here," the training officer said. And with the deft move of a veteran, the cop spun him around and cuffed him in one effortless motion.

"What are you doing?" Rothmiller asked him.

"We're arresting him for malicious mischief."

"For breaking the window?" Rothmiller said. "But we didn't see him do it." According to the book, all they had so far was a report. There was insufficient evidence for an arrest.

"Oh, I saw it," the trainer said. "Didn't you see it?"

"No," the rookie said.

"No, here's what happened," the training officer insisted. "We got the call, we pulled up, and saw this guy throw the potted plant through the window. That's what we saw!"

Just for added emphasis, he yelled up to the woman, "Hey, he threw that potted plant through your window, didn't he?"

The woman yelled agreement.

Then the training officer turned to Rothmiller and in measured tones said, "See? She saw it. We saw it. That's the end of it."

And that's the way the arrest report was written.

Lying on arrest reports was routine in felony cases as well. If a cop rolled up to a burglary, saw a screen off the window and a suspect walking across the lawn, his report would state he saw the suspect climbing out the window.

Unfriendly witnesses could throw a wrench into these twisted reports, but if the arresting officer left their names and accounts off the arrest report, then even if the public defender knew such witnesses existed, it would be up to the attorney to find their location. This was a virtual impossibility given the number of active cases in each public defender's file.

Again and again Rothmiller watched cops decide for themselves who was guilty, and then weave a spell over the arrest report to make it match their perceptions. Most of the arrest reports he encountered were doctored in some way—facts deleted or invented. It wasn't exactly the frontier justice of a lynch mob, but it wasn't justice either. It was just the way things worked.

And this bogus reporting wasn't confined to just the inefficient bunglers on the force. Over and over, Rothmiller saw, the more proficient the officer, the more sophisticated were his false accounts. Defense attorneys could rarely shake the testimony of a polite, earnest, diligent, *lying* cop.

Officers, seeing the crush of everyday crime, believed they were under siege, that extralegal procedures were necessary to counter all those constitutional rights guaranteed to the enemy. If the suspect happened to be innocent of this crime, then he was no doubt guilty of another one anyway, so it was better to guarantee a conviction when you had the chance.

Cops generally didn't debate the philosophical rights or wrongs of filing false reports and offering perjured testimony. But they were forced to discuss the specifics of their arrest tales with each other because often these were communal undertakings.

Every officer concerned was drawn into an inner circle to ensure all testimony was in agreement. The arresting officer would say, "Here's what happened," and everyone would confirm that scenario.

If it helped the case, he might even ask an officer who was in fact a witness not to see what he saw. In such an instance the arresting cop would say, "Look, you pulled up late and didn't see anything, correct?" And that's the way the second officer would tell it.

Claiming a suspect appeared to be on PCP (angel dust) was a classic communal tale, and one used in the defense of Rodney King's LAPD attackers. The public had been primed repeatedly with frightening stories about the sometimes superhuman strength displayed by PCP zombies. So cops knew that suspicion of a PCP high would often work as a handy excuse for tearing into an unarmed suspect.

There was nothing else to do, the cops would say. We were attacked by some kind of Godzilla who'd evidently swallowed an evil secret formula. (Tests administered to King the night of his arrest showed he was legally drunk, but there was no trace of PCP in his system.)

A suspect who ran was in big trouble. Unofficial LAPD policy has long been to punish a rabbit, period. Whether he's on foot or in a vehicle, the suspect better halt. If he ran, he paid. Streetwise toughs generally knew this. Consequently, there weren't as many hot pursuits. Runners had to ask themselves: Is this really worth it?

Suspects who did run were even more desperate to get away and avoid the beating they assumed was waiting at the end of an unsuccessful getaway. This raised the danger quotient several notches for the suspect, the pursuing cops, and any innocent bystanders.

Meanwhile, the rule remained in force. You ran, you paid. It was part of the give-and-take between cops and (perceived) creeps.

The policy was hammered home to Rothmiller one night outside a tough housing project below Baldwin Hills. Cops referred to this predominantly black area as "the jungle." After a young suspect led a pack of officers on a lengthy chase through the buildings, he was finally cornered in a very narrow alley. The cops' adrenaline was pumping, and the kid, breathing hard, looked around desperately for a friendly face.

"Okay, okay, okay, I give up," he said, now utterly submissive.

An officer charged through the crowd of blue shirts and ordered the kid to turn around and put his hands on the wall.

Then he decided to give the kid counsel: "You don't fuckin' run from the police!" He punctuated this information with an overhand baton chop to the head. Bam! The kid was down. A swarm of cops moved forward as though on command.

Rothmiller saw an automatic, almost involuntary response at work, an instinct ingrained into the psyche of the dozen or so officers after years of training and peer pressure. Fortunately for the kid, the alley was so cramped only three or four cops actually delivered blows.

Fortunately for the officers, no one was around with a video camera.

LAPD cops, even when they disliked each other, always drew together against outsiders. This meant the level of violence perpetrated by any two cops or group of cops tended to sink to the lowest common denominator within their gathering.

This wasn't something Rothmiller discovered all at once. It was a gradual learning process with occasional blasts of discovery. He learned rules were bent, rules were broken, and that rules weren't what the rules said.

At the academy, instructors had besieged recruits with the dictum that they must protect their partner. *Never let your partner down.* Out on the street, that formula was transmuted into a stronger, far more demanding code. Like the ethic of Hell's Angels or Crips or Outlaws, there was the code of the blue tribe.

When one acted, *all must follow.* That meant if a fellow warrior lashed out at someone, the others were expected to join in. This was a rite. A way to seal the bond over and over. Us against them. You found out what the beef was later.

Out on patrol, Rothmiller and a partner for the night made a traffic stop of a young white male. The driver was cocky: "What the fuck did I do?" Rothmiller's partner asked for identification and the young man pulled out his wallet. Just as it cleared his back pocket, the partner plowed him under with a baton blow.

Rothmiller hadn't spotted any transgression, but by reflex he lashed out with a blow of his own. It was a Pavlovian response that had been shocked into his consciousness. You didn't ask questions, you finished it.

They cuffed the suspect, now bloodied. "What happened?" Rothmiller asked.

"Furtive move," grinned the partner, extracting a standard cop phrase from his mental notebook. "I didn't like the prick's attitude," he added, which was in an unwritten, far more compelling manual of behavior.

There must be a point somewhere where one says: Enough! But where was that point supposed to be? These cops were not all wicked men and women. Some of them were good-humored, friendly, helpful human beings. They certainly weren't concentration camp guards molded into malicious brutes by evil state propaganda.

But their tolerance for antisocial behavior by their peers gradually increased, first, through the powerful process that started inside the academy. And then, through continued reinforcement during their LAPD careers.

When no one complained, when no one exclaimed that these were extraordinary patterns of conduct, when everything around a recruit told that individual that this was the norm, it became normal. It was the dialect of the street. You took some crap and you gave some back and maybe it would all balance out.

In this work that entailed very real danger, it was imperative to be accepted and trusted by fellow cops. Work wasn't just work and it wasn't just social, either. The challenges posed by patrolling America's urban landscape were not just topics for cocktail chatter. They were life and death.

Standard comportment didn't seem to cover situations the cops encountered. Over the years, through unwritten replies to questions most citizens never had to address, the LAPD had formed its own system of answers.

The "furtive move" excuse, the beatings that awaited runners, the entire phalanx of special situations demanding blue justice right there on the street were all prompted by one generic crime: *contempt of cop*. This was similar to the code of conduct followed by L.A. street gangs. If one "dis-es" (disrespects) a gang-banger, one must expect retribution.

Contempt of cop was something easily grasped in the gang territories of L.A., where kindred spirits shared kindred philosophies. To the gang-bangers, the unwritten rulebook governing the crime of contempt of cop was just another grim reality of their mean streets. Of course it raised the level of rage and despair, but they could live with it.

Just as street gangs accepted and sheltered and treasured the absolute psychos among their ranks, so did the LAPD fraternity. Some loonies did manage to bluff their way through the department's psychological screenings. And everyone knew who they were.

These were crazies whose ultimate goal was to waste someone, lunatics who liked nothing better than to inflict pain. They were always on the lookout for the slightest provocation.

The psychos were the cops in the locker room who always suited up like gladiators. Instead of the normal sidearm and concealed backup gun that most officers carried, the wackos often carried three or more weapons, including a large folding knife in a sheath on their Sam Brown belts. A big buck knife on an officer's belt was a sure sign of a goofball. These men weren't out there to keep the streets safe. They were looking for ways to precipitate violence.

As a rookie, Rothmiller wondered at first why so many street toughs were willing to attack groups of cops when the odds were so clearly against them.

Then he learned the secret. Early on he saw a fellow cop pat down a suspect. "Don't move!" the cop ordered: And then almost immediately the young black man jumped and took a swing at the cop. The guy was nuts, Rothmiller thought, meat on a hook. And all the cops in range tenderized him. Then Rothmiller wondered if the cop had pulled something. He did, didn't he?

"You got it, rookie," another cop explained.

The frisker, Rothmiller learned, kept a pin hidden in his Sam Brown belt. Right after he told the man not to move, the cop jabbed him. So the witnesses across the street had all seen the detained suspect suddenly jump and swing wildly—just moments after he was told, in no uncertain terms, not to move.

Rothmiller learned to recognize this favorite psycho trick. The nutsos seemed to have their own pain network. Sometimes they just pinched the target in the scrotum or in the sensitive area under the armpits. Same result.

Or the psycho would simply flick the enemy in the eye with his index finger. This worked particularly well when the target was seated in a car. It was a move so subtle not even passengers in the car would be aware of what sparked the altercation.

Once the fight began, there were plenty of other dirty tricks that were creative leaps beyond the mere employment of saps (blackjacks) or batons—bending fingers back, twisting ears, tightening handcuffs into medieval torture devices, slamming the victim's head into the door while placing him in a vehicle.

The textbook-versus-reality teaching method at the academy also extended to compliance holds—an assortment of pain-inducing arm twists, wrist bends, and finger jams that wouldn't appear violent to the casual observer. Academy instructors taught recruits to use this array of inducements on uncooperative suspects, but there were also hints they could be used as well on arrestees who were merely irritating. In those cases, compliance holds were not merely inducements but forms of torture.

Any viewers of late-night news in Los Angeles and many other cities have undoubtedly seen compliance holds without realizing it. If they paid attention to the way the suspect was walking, they might see the individual dancing up on tiptoe—"climbing the sky"—because of the very real sensation of wrists or fingers near the breaking point.

Or they could look for a cop with his index finger under someone's nose, another extremely subtle yet very effective method of torture-compliance.

Rothmiller knew cops who liked to take a vocal suspect to jail with duct tape over his mouth. The cop would hold his nose just long enough to make him think about dying. Or they would place the victim facedown on the patrol unit's floor, cuffed with both hand and ankle restraints, the officer's boot firmly on his neck. On the ride back, the cop's hands would be in full view. Meanwhile, he would grind the victim's face slowly into the floormat.

If the driver of a paddy wagon had some grievance against his human cargo, he didn't need much imagination to make their lives miserable. They were handcuffed and seated on unpadded, wooden benches along the side. The rest of their environment: bare metal. The driver would simply brake sharply and the offenders would vault forward like so many human cannonballs. Then, when the gas was applied, the effect would be repeated in reverse.

Rothmiller saw passengers of such rides when they reached the station—covered with bruises, barely able to walk or talk.

Mace also expanded opportunities for malicious cops, although most officers generally disfavored the use for which it was intended. True, it would probably incapacitate the victim through the miracle of chemical misery, but it also left behind a nonselective foul residue that might irritate the arresting officer or his partner, either through direct contact with the suspect or with the patrol car that eventually transported him to jail.

Some LAPD officers would employ Mace and CS gas canisters in ways not designed by their manufacturers. A favorite ploy, usually used against cruising gang members, began after the cops pulled a customary roust. The car was pulled over and the victims were ordered out.

Then, after a routine shakedown, one officer told the victims to face away from their vehicle while his partner made what appeared to be a casual inspection of the passenger compartment. Actually, the officer was deftly spraying gas in the dashboard air-conditioning vents and across the grill. One quick spray was all it took, especially in summer.

The cops would leave, the homeboys would pile back in the vehicle, start the engine, and the cops would have the last laugh.

Punishing underage homeboys required a certain degree of creativity because their tender years made them nearly invulnerable to serious prosecution. Also, the kids considered bookings and police records badges of honor. They merely bolstered the gang-bangers' street reputation. And seriously beating a minor was too likely to provoke a serious in-house investigation.

Rothmiller knew some officers who caught a quadraplegic homeboy and his sister who were burglarizing their neighbors' homes, using their duplex apartment as a convenient base of operations. The boy had earlier been crippled by a drive-by shooting. Confined to a wheelchair, he would serve as lookout while his sister went in after the loot.

The officers, finding a cache of stereo parts and other goods in the apartment, arrested the sister and took her to jail. But the quadraplegic posed a problem. If the cops arrested him, they would have to take him to the hospital and endure hours of bureaucratic hassles. Mountains of paperwork were required whenever they arrested a handicapped suspect.

The homeboy knew he was practically invulnerable to the legal system, knew that by arresting him the cops would suffer more than he would, knew that if he ended up in court he would look like a helpless victim and his arresting officers like heartless monsters. So to make matters worse, he mocked the officers, daring them to take him in. *Contempt of cop.*

The cops, desperate to do something about this flagrant breach of street ethics, finally realized that the boy's mother wouldn't be home from work for hours. So they parked his chair in the middle of a room and locked one wheel. It was the only kind of street justice they could think of at the moment.

Methods ranged all the way from practical jokes to serious beatings and unjustified shootings. Practitioners of street justice ranged from sadistic cops who looked for ways to hurt people every workday of their lives to relatively level-headed cops who indulged in extralegal punishment only in scattered instances.

Cops believed the general public would support their thin blue line in a good many of these practices, even though they might not necessarily want to know the details. The Los Angeles community wanted criminals kept at bay, and it didn't want to pay a lot of taxes. What citizens got was a relatively small paramilitary police force whose officers played by their own rules.

Because no officer was completely innocent, a communal shield mechanism was in force to protect even the worst offenders. Even-tempered cops never knew when they might go over the edge momentarily or just make a mistake. In that case they would need chits in the bank.

But beyond that reality was the sterner dictum that a cop could never rat out another cop. If he did, he would be like Yasser Arafat trying to survive in the Israeli army. It wouldn't work. A whistleblower would be snuffed out before he got his lips puckered.

Even when other cops were disgusted by the psychos, they would never turn them in. Besides, in the LAPD socialization process, the psychos' genes were dominant. Their methods were more likely to rub off on the rational cops than the other way around. It was all part of the dynamic by which the capacity for violence sank to the lowest common denominator within any particular circle of cops.

The only way to mount a protest was from outside—quit and then yell your head off. But even among ex-cops, loyalty to the code was stronger than Krazy Glue. Officers increasingly uncomfortable with the way things worked counted off the days to retirement and went about feeling vaguely uneasy. Like someone once said, what you want and what you get don't always come on the same bus.

As time went by, Rothmiller saw cops demand information in a variety of ways. Sometimes they dangled suspects by their ankles from the edge of buildings, reminiscent of the old helicopter-dangling scenes that occurred during the Vietnam War. This trick would often be executed while a pack of cop onlookers joked and made bets about whether the victim looked like a bouncer or a splatterer. Telling these jokes was the job of the onlookers. If they weren't danglers, they were supposed to do their part as official chortlers.

As for the victim, perhaps in his mind he might figure that the obviously crazy cops holding him wouldn't really drop him. How could they explain it away? But even if they didn't intend to waste him, they might lose their grip, which is what the cops were yelling down to the victim. Meanwhile every cell in the victim's body is screaming to be pulled back to safety. Invariably the rest of the body would win out over what his mind tried to tell him. "I'll talk! I'll talk!"

The dangling trick was just one of a number of

practices that might be called practical jokes. At least the cop perpetrators liked to think of them as jokes. They ranged across a broad spectrum, from boorish pranks into deep pathological territory. All these frolics shared an underlying philosophy— that officers were on the streets as an occupying force. The civilians were enemies to be subdued.

In the Wilshire division, along about 3 or 4 A.M. on the morning watch, there would be six or seven patrol cars out there filled with bored officers. Sometimes they played follow the leader. A lead car would tear through streets, alleys, and parking lots at speeds up to 90 miles an hour, and everyone had to follow. Although this fraternity-type chase could of course injure or kill a bystander, it wasn't designed to hurt anyone. It was one of the more innocent pranks.

There were countless times officers in a patrol car would zip past a group of minority youngsters hanging out on a corner. One patrolman would lean out the window, aiming a baton like a rifle, then the driver would switch the ignition off and back on in a flash. The big power train of an engine would backfire and the civilians, thinking they were under attack, would scatter like chickens. This always seemed to work best in a Plymouth, making it the preferred patrol vehicle.

Then there was the "Diamond Formation," also pulled on the night shift by restless officers who were out there when even the criminals were asleep. A half-dozen or so patrol cars would meet at a prearranged side street off the expansively wide Olympic Boulevard, usually around Highland. There they would wait for a mark—a lone driver on the lonely boulevard. One car would pull out in front of the chosen vehicle and then proceed at a pace of 25 miles an hour. Of course the intended victim would slow down.

Then two more patrol cars would pull up on

either side of the victim and squeeze closer. A fourth would pull up behind, tailgating the victim into a neat box. Any extra cars would then join in and make a fuller, tighter formation.

All cops in the cars would turn and stare at their victim, giving him no instructions. This driver could not slow down or speed up. He could not know what was expected of him. He could only continue on helplessly. Eventually, when the cops were through toying with him, the formation leader would bark an order over the radio, and all cars would break off at once in prearranged directions, just like the Blue Angel fighter jocks they were mimicking.

Rothmiller saw the Diamond Formation pulled five or six times. Each time, when it was finished, the victim of the carefully engineered surreal experience would stop his vehicle and sit there in the middle of the street, too shaken to go on. In the racially mixed neighborhood where this trick was often played, persons of any race might come down the street. But Rothmiller never saw the Diamond Formation pulled on anyone but black men.

Then there was the "lie detector test," again administered in the middle of the night. This one was always pulled on some lone pedestrian. The cops would wait until they could find some poor soul with a clearly limited education. They would determine this after questioning him about his identity, where he was going, and the like. The more innocent his answers the better.

"Bullshit," a cop would say. "You're not telling the truth." If he had identification, they would say it was phony. "Tell us the truth, goddammit!"

Then, after they yelled at him awhile, someone would say, "Okay, we're going to administer a lie detector test. You know what that is?"

"Yeah."

Then they would hand the victim a specially

prepared traffic flare covered with electrical tape and attached to a fearsome-looking battery.

"This is a special one, though. You lie, you die. You drop it, you die." Then the cops would get behind the patrol car as though they feared an explosion and begin asking questions. When he heard a click, they told him, that meant he'd answered untruthfully, and he had thirty seconds to back up and tell the truth. Or go up in smoke. The cops could induce a click by keying the mike on the public address system of their patrol car.

"What's your name?"

He would answer.

"What's your address?"

Answer.

"You ever sucked a dick?"

"No."

Click.

"Jesus, it clicked. You've got thirty seconds to tell the truth."

"No, honest, never. I never sucked a dick!"

"Ten seconds."

"No, never! I swear!"

"Okay, I guess it must have malfunctioned. It seems okay for now. Now where were you born?"

And so it would go until the cops tired of their joke. Rothmiller saw the "lie detector" pulled twice. The first time, at least for a while, the rookie assumed the victim must be just playing along with the prank. But by the time the cops were through with this man, he was deathly scared. It was no joke to him. The second victim was equally terrified. Both men were black.

· 3 ·

Contempt
of Cop

A^t the academy, Rothmiller and his classmates learned over and over that the greatest
test awaited them on the street, that it would
determine their career path for their entire tenure
as police officers. Eventually they all came to learn
that this "test" referred to was no generic process
of day-to-day police work. Their instructors were
talking about facing down the enemy and then
laying into him.

"Are you going to kick ass or stand back when
asked to assist another officer in a physical altercation?" one instructor asked them in an accusing
tone.

The answer had to be delivered in deeds, not
words, and any probationer who had yet to prove
himself would receive a multitude of unsubtle
reminders from his training officer that he remained a fight virgin, a cherry who must still prove
himself to the blue grapevine.

The idea was to find a fight and then wade in like
a cop from hell. It was of course better to win, but

even if the rookie lost, he could score points for tearing into his prey like a badger after a grizzly. That was what the veterans wanted to see.

But there was yet another element to this rite of passage, twenty-one-year-old Rothmiller learned. Not only would he have to kick someone's ass, and soon, it had better be a black man. Aside from their very real prejudice toward blacks, veteran officers also recognized one very salient fact about white people: most were afraid of blacks. So taking on a white man, unless he were some kind of Marciano, just wouldn't be enough. The vets wanted to see how a rookie would respond to a black man in his face.

At this point a rookie had three choices:

1. *He could ignore the taunting and go his own way.* In that case he would earn a "jacket" that would follow him around his entire LAPD career; this guy is afraid to mix it up. He can't be trusted. Give him the cold shoulder, and if he ever gets in physical jeopardy, look the other way.

2. *Complain to a higher authority.* Impossible. In the first place, the authorities knew all about this ritual, and they clearly didn't disapprove. In the second place, the rookie received only strong hints, not orders. There were no grounds for complaint. And in the third place, this was a powerless probationer. If he became an early pain, he was easy to ignore, easy to fire. He carried no weight in the intradepartmental justice system.

Everyone hates a coward. But now this rookie would have a jacket with not one but two names on it: coward and snitch. He would be friendless, alone, despised, not long in the department.

3. *He could go along.* Not a pretty alternative, to be sure. Especially to a rookie with scruples and a conscience to nag him when he didn't live up to them. But then there were an awful lot of nasties out there begging to be thumped. Why not just bide

your time a bit, wait for a truly deserving dirtbag, and then get it over with once and for all? Because, after all, options one and two were no options at all.

That was the reality of the LAPD socialization process. Previous standards had to give way to the standards of the tribe, with no room for renegades.

One night probationer Rothmiller and his training officer were called to a domestic dispute in a black neighborhood. Following routine, they separated the combatants. They walked the husband behind a detached garage. As so often happened in these cases, the man turned his anger on the police. Why was this any of their business anyway? He became increasingly abusive and even put his hands on Rothmiller, shoving him.

The training officer calmly leaned against the garage door, acting like he was observing the dullest of chess matches. Finally, he said, "Are you going to let this guy keep chipping away like this? What are you going to do about it?"

Rothmiller hesitated. Was this the time? And just then his training officer added: "I think it's time."

Rothmiller attacked, lunging furiously at this lamb provided by providence. He worked him into a chokehold and, his adrenal glands pumping, dragged him all around the yard, kneeing him in the back and the kidneys, teaching him who ruled this jungle. Finally, the probationer wrenched the man's arms behind him and cuffed him. There, it was done.

"Good job," the training officer smiled. "You did good."

When a rookie brought in his handcuffed proof of passage, it was like a hunter bringing in a twelve-point buck. Other officers admired the handiwork, looking for telltale bruises and assessing the size of the quarry. And the training officer sang his praises. Within hours, everyone in the station knew he had proved himself, reinforcing the warrior ritual. It wasn't pretty, but that's the way it was, and that's the way it happened to Rothmiller.

An officer had to repeat this rite whenever he was transferred to another division. Regardless of years of service, he had to once again prove his willingness to kick butt in order to reassure his new street partners.

Contempt of cop rules differed for women antagonists, Rothmiller learned, but only by degree. For instance, it was standard practice for cops who had to deal with such an offender to throw her around by the hair. This was particularly effective when the cop removed her from her vehicle. If she'd kept going after being signaled to stop, this was just as much of a personal affront to the police as any delivered by a male. It demanded extralegal response. You ran, you paid.

Of course the rules didn't apply exactly the same way to citizens whose word might provoke serious inquiry and possibly even be accepted by higher authorities. Rothmiller noticed that cops, by and large, were excellent judges of somebody's socioeconomic standing. And in those rare cases when bigwig citizens ran afoul of the contempt of cop statutes, just booking them was usually sufficient punishment anyway. They had a much lower threshold of tolerance for the holding tank.

Those whose place was closer to the bottom tiers of respectability were more apt to see an arrest as just part of the brutal world around them, an annoyance that must be suffered from time to time.

What confused the process was the occasional entanglement with a middle-class black in casual attire. This confusion of race and class stereotypes could make for a serious mistake. Staunch middle-class citizens didn't expect to be frisked, for instance, for routine traffic violations. Especially when there hadn't been any violation. Most especially when the friskee was black and he knew in his heart of hearts that none of this would be happening if his skin were a different hue.

These instances were so numerous that black males from every background and every neighborhood in Los Angeles were repeatedly subjected to harassment. And they united black criminals and black victims in their contempt for police.

In March 1988, ex-major leaguer Joe Morgan, walking through the Los Angeles airport, was grabbed by the neck, thrown to the floor, and handcuffed by LAPD officers. Mistaken identity, the cops said. That will be $540,000, a jury told the City of Los Angeles. In 1991, the city lost $14,685,000 in excessive force settlements, judgments, and awards. That was up from $891,000 in 1980.

In 1990, ex-Laker Jamaal Wilkes complained after LAPD cops hauled him from his car and handcuffed him. Well, the department said, the light over his license plate was burned out. But every black man in L.A. knew his real crime. Wilkes drove through a white neighborhood in a nice car. *Suspicious behavior.*

Ironically, the possibility of a baton beating increased in Los Angeles because of a public furor over police brutality. In 1982, after a series of blacks died from police chokeholds, the police commission banned their use. It was in the midst of that furor that Chief Gates made what was to become one of his most ill-famed remarks. He said that perhaps blacks were more likely to suffer chokehold deaths than "normal" people.

Although chokeholds were no doubt used too liberally by L.A. police, the new ruling shrank the cops' arsenal of responses, making batons the weapon of choice for nonlethal combat. Although only a few deaths might be linked directly to baton use, the move from baton to firearm became more common and much faster.

This might be part of the explanation—but only a part—for the fact is that Los Angeles police have been found to be the nation's most trigger-happy. The Christopher Commission, appointed to study these matters after the King beating, reported that LAPD cops killed 3 people and wounded 8.1 for every 1,000 officers in 1986.

Detroit, which came in second, ranked a very distant second, with 1.2 killed and 5 wounded.

"Death to the enemy" has long been a quiet but very real slogan of the police force that invented SWAT teams. The LAPD's tolerance for killing could be discerned from top to bottom. The message from Chief Gates seemed to encourage a year-round hunting season. The chief (whose son is a drug addict) said, for example, that "casual drug users ought to be taken out and shot." Such utterances from the mouths of, say, shock-radio hosts, might not be so terribly alarming. But when they came from the chief of a major urban police force, they set a tone of acceptance whose consequences were real death on real streets.

Meanwhile, as recruits became socialized within the LAPD fraternity, they learned that the surest ticket to respect among their peers was to kill somebody. Despite the department's protestations to the contrary, officers and homeboys secured a rep the same way. Taking down an opponent was a badge of honor. Both groups no doubt likened themselves to fighter pilots who lined up representations of their dogfight kills on the fuselage.

Some cops, particularly SWAT team snipers, actually wore badges of their kills by cutting off the bottom of the spent shell casing used in the shooting and wearing it as a lapel pin. The practice was winked at by those in charge.

Cops loved to tell the world how dangerous their

work was. But traversing dark yards or alleys in his work, Rothmiller always felt safer in uniform. Civilian clothes were just a target for trigger-happy LAPD cops looking to secure a reputation.

One night, while still a green probationer, Rothmiller was ordered to hit the streets under the tutelage of a patrolman two. This man was not an official training officer, who was always at least a patrolman three. But the training officers were otherwise engaged, and so another veteran was thrown into the breach to give Rothmiller guidance for the night.

Later on in the shift, during the early hours of the morning, when there were no eyes and ears on the street, the veteran officer saw a black man walking along Olympic Boulevard. The cop braked in the middle of the deserted street. "Hey, you!" he called out.

The man looked around. "Who? Me?"

"See how they always look around like that?" the cop told Rothmiller. "Who the hell else would I be talking to?" Then, to the pedestrian, the cop yelled: "Get your ass over here!"

The man walked up to the driver's door.

"What are you doing here?"

"Walking home, officer. I just got off work."

"Why don't you drive?"

"I don't have a car, so I walk."

So far this was what the LAPD would call a proactive patrol tactic. Pull up and look at the guy's teeth. See what he's up to. This man looked very much to Rothmiller like a legitimate citizen walking home from his job. Some poor guy who was working the same cruddy hours as Rothmiller, only for less pay. He was due an apology and farewell. But it was not to be.

"I want you running from now on," Rothmiller's partner said.

"What?"

"I don't ever want to see you walking. I want you running down this street. Now put your hand down here." The cop pointed to the metal frame of the open window. "Go on, put your hand down there or I'll run your ass in!"

The citizen gingerly placed his hand down on the frame.

In one motion the cop pulled his baton off the seat and came down across the knuckles like a woodsman wielding his ax. As hard as he could.

The man cried with pain, bending back and forth and cradling his injured hand with the other. Rothmiller sat in revulsion, not completely sure he'd seen what he thought he had seen. Something must have broken in that hand. And it still wasn't over.

"All right. Get your ass over here and put your other hand down!"

"No, please, you're gonna break my hand," the man pleaded.

"You heard me. Get your ass over here! Put down that other hand!"

The man, crying, cringing, placed his good hand on the window frame. To do this, he had to have a very educated understanding of what lay in store if he disobeyed.

Bam! Second hand smashed, too.

"That'll teach you not to pull away when I tell you to put your hand down," the cop said, satisfied now. "Now get your ass out of here. Run, goddammit!"

The victim, enveloped in what could only be excrutiating pain and terror, ran. What else could he do? He ran.

"Faster, goddammit! I said run!" The cop followed the man for a block, pouring on just a little more mental torture. Then he peeled off.

Laughing, the cop turned to his rookie partner.

"You're not going to tell anybody about this," he said. It was both a statement and a question.

Rothmiller knew what this meant, knew no supervisor would take the word of a probationer over a senior officer. The mere attempt to report this would give him a jacket he could never overcome. No more job. And this bastard would stay on the street.

He could also quit. But if everyone sane who wanted to work fairly abandoned the department to the maniacs, he wasn't sure it would be helpful anyway. Rothmiller thought about his bills and obligations. He thought about the six months he'd already spent in the academy, his time on the street, the years he'd put into college, the plans he'd made. Should he throw it all away?

Those were big questions. He was only twenty-one years old. He answered them by hunkering down. He kept his mouth shut and his ass out of trouble. But he thought about what he'd just seen.

He thought about the victim who surely knew better than any Supreme Court justice just how relevant was the Bill of Rights to a black man at 4 A.M. on the streets of L.A.

What would this man think about his country now? What would he teach his children and their children? Would they revere the Founding Fathers who counted their ancestors as three-fifths of a white person?

This was several years after Martin Luther King, Jr., was shot dead. A decade since his "I have a dream" speech. What would this policeman's victim dream about now? Could he continue to share King's dream? Or had he lost it long ago anyway in similar incidents?

That man and his family weren't living in the same America as the majority of its citizens. They were living in a police state—a Los Angeles Police

Department state that closed ranks around its torturers and psychopaths and protected them.

It was instructive that this cop had chosen an innocent man as his victim. He could have waited to torture a purse snatcher or a stickup man or a rapist, but he deliberately picked a victim that made his sadism even harder to understand. It was as though he understood that by choosing this particular victim, the story would be even more unbelievable. He would be that much safer.

As the nights followed the terrible night on Olympic Boulevard, Rothmiller could be thankful for only one thing. At least the victim, whoever he was, didn't try to file a complaint. If he did, then Rothmiller, according to the code of silence, would have been called upon to back up the psycho cop.

Someday Rothmiller could even be put in a position where he would have to help this sadistic lunatic in a tight situation. He resolved that in his own duties he would never start a fight with a citizen. In his tenure as a patrolman he would use his baton perhaps a half-dozen times, but never because he struck first.

But then there were times when he showed up to help a cop in a fight, plunged in, and then found out later the cop was just another goon who'd provoked an incident. He tried to believe there was nothing he could do about it. A cop took care of business, then got the facts later. That's the way it was if he wanted to work alongside other cops.

A few years later, Rothmiller was himself a training officer working out of the Northeast division and it was his turn to grade the courage of a raw probationer. They were dispatched late one night to a dispute at an apartment complex. For some reason, the female manager of the apartments had used her passkey to enter a tenant's apartment unannounced, sparking the row.

After interviewing the upset woman tenant,

Rothmiller and his rookie moved down the hallway to speak with the woman manager, who was accompanied by a man in his twenties and the man's mother. Rothmiller had learned to try to defuse and sort out such situations by showing a calm, controlled demeanor. But suddenly, without warning, the man and the manager pushed him back and slammed the door in his face, injuring his foot.

None of this seemed reasonable, but it was all a typical escalation of rage and idiocy within the angry, destitute climes of the City of Angels. And it was one that no cop could ignore. A quick turn of events that turned the night from boredom to dread to senseless violence.

This particular eruption of violence happened to be an assault on a police officer—a felony. No more time for talk. Rothmiller switched to Plan B and began banging his nightstick against the hollow-core door. After about ten strokes he'd created a large enough hole to see the three people inside trying to barricade the door with furniture.

"Call the police!" he yelled over to the woman tenant. "Tell them an officer needs help!"

Rothmiller kicked through the door and was immediately jumped by three adversaries. As the two women heaved lamps, bottles, and several other household items at him that he didn't have time to catalog, Rothmiller tried targeting the most dangerous of the threesome, the man, with his sap and baton. But each moment the cop was in deeper trouble from the freestyle barrage.

In a corner of his mind, Rothmiller wondered where his partner was. He more or less assumed his rookie had been felled by these dirtbags, because he was nowhere to be seen. Finally Rothmiller managed to get hold of the man's belt buckle with one hand and a fistful of collar with the other. He lifted him, stepping back for a body slam—and slipped on a soda bottle. Rothmiller fell flat on his back.

The women took this opportunity to begin stomping him. Swinging at their legs, the cop looked up to see this night wasn't getting any better. The man was hoisting a reclining chair over his head to bring it down on Rothmiller. Time to shoot. Rothmiller reached for his pistol, but found that a table leg had wedged his holster shut. The La-Z-Boy came down on target. Splat!

Fortunately for Rothmiller, the threesome decided it was now time to make an exit. All this had transpired in perhaps a minute or so. Looking up, Rothmiller finally spotted his partner standing in the doorway, the tag team coming at him. The rookie came to life, turned, and ran out before anyone reached him.

Rothmiller struggled to his feet, ran down one floor to street level, and made it to his patrol car. There was no probationer in sight. He quickly radioed for help, but it wasn't necessary. The tenant had followed his instructions, and the first troop of the Northeast division cavalry showed up in time to collar all three assailants.

The gang of rescuers was fuming because the three offenders had dared to ignore their orders to halt. Then, when the arriving officers took one look at the torn and battered Rothmiller, they knew they were dealing here with a serious case of contempt of cop. There were no witnesses, no video cameras to record the brutal consequences, which consisted mostly of Mickey Mantle baton whacks across the shins of the transgressors.

About this time, Rothmiller passed out. When he came around at the hospital, he asked: "Where in the hell was my partner?"

According to the two officers who arrived first, they saw the rookie tearing down the street like a greyhound. Assuming he was in foot pursuit of the perpetrators, they followed. But eventually they realized this guy was just running, period. Fleeing the scene because he was so frightened he didn't know what else to do.

Just as the police grapevine heralds someone's admission into the cop fraternity, it also quickly transmits the accounts of those who fail. And like most bad news, the story gains embellishments with time. A recovered Rothmiller lobbied for the rookie's dismissal, but the wheels of departmental justice ground slightly in the probationer's favor. Instead, he was turned into one of the countless stationbound flunkies who push their pencils around a desk somewhere beneath a slowly ticking clock. He became the exception to prove the rule—a known coward who survived and, in his own way, eventually thrived. He became a sergeant.

But years later, the story of the rookie who ran was being told and retold. New probationers were still cruising past to view him at his work station like some kind of diseased ape in a pink dress on view in a cage. And the rookies were warned: don't trust this coward.

Where did women officers fit in this macho world of ass-kickers? They were generally lumped somewhere below the vicinity of "mouse meat," a male officer who just didn't have the physical size or strength to crack heads properly. Female cops weren't expected to win fights, but they were expected to make an attempt, to show they were willing to mix it up.

Beyond this, women cops were valued in certain tense situations because they tended to have keener patience and verbal ability. They were more apt to employ the kind of mothering skills that certain savvy male veterans could bring forth to tone things down. But the fact remained that lots of male cops were leery of partnering with a woman because of the consensus that during a tussle, someone might easily get her gun away from her.

But for all its dangers, disappointments, and

headaches, the street, as so many cops learned, was a magnet, a fascinating urbanscape that kept cops coming back for more. They hated it and loved it and experienced it night after night as an explorer might stalk new territories. And they went by rules no one wrote out and everybody understood.

As time went by, Rothmiller learned to notice things other people couldn't see, to deal with situations most people never knew existed. He earned respect from fellow cops and citizens and scumbags. He had been taken in by the LAPD as one of its own. He was uncomfortable with part of the blue world around him but unwilling to surrender all of it in some failed attempt to change a part of it.

After eighteen months in patrol in the Wilshire division he did a stint in community relations, giving antirape talks, encouraging neighborhood watch committees, acting as a spokesman to the news media.

Very few citizens cared to go to more than one neighborhood watch meeting because Rothmiller and the other speakers were ordered to deliver the same crime prevention hints at each session. But the LAPD hierarchy, then under Chief Ed Davis, wanted to see attendance figures rising. So Rothmiller and the others were ordered to hand out free ice cream cones in school playgrounds. Each kid who took a cone was counted as an attendee.

"It stinks," agreed the lieutenant, "but we have to do it this way," a credo that might have been engraved above the door of LAPD headquarters.

· 4 ·

Undercover
Justice

After working as a training officer for eighteen months, patrol officer Rothmiller went "on loan" to other units, where he did detective work investigating car-theft and burglary rings and doing his time in the vice unit. There he eventually came to specialize in taking down various gambling and bookmaking operations, but he also did his time working the sex detail, arresting suspects for prostitution, lewd conduct, and related sundry acts.

While he was working vice, Officer Frank McManus, a friend assigned to burglary, was given a peculiar case. Someone was stealing sculptures and other forms of artwork that decorated resting places in Forest Lawn, the sprawling cemetery that was once the butt of some Johnny Carson jokes.

Forest Lawn, which sat on a huge tract of land, straddled the cities of Los Angeles and suburban Glendale. Since few crimes were reported at cemeteries, at first no one knew who had jurisdiction over the graveyard capers. But eventually it was determined that the crimes were being committed in an L.A. section, and Rothmiller's friend got the case.

McManus received information that a particular individual was either an actual perpetrator or at least had information on the Forest Lawn thefts. The suspect's address was unknown, but the cop also found out that a second individual, whose whereabouts were known, might have information on the man's location. It was typical of the chain of tips, facts, and guesswork that made up detective work.

This second individual was known to cops as a very much out-of-the-closet gay who was part of the L.A. underworld fringe. Rothmiller's friend was just about to go over and try to get some information from the man when Rothmiller got a brainstorm.

"Don't tell the guy you're a cop," he said. "Just act like a friend who's trying to get ahold of his friend."

"Won't work," said the plainclothes officer, who was dressed in standard detective attire. "He'd be on to me in a second."

Just then a woman officer walked in the room. She was dressed in sequined jeans and a halter top. "I don't think so," Rothmiller answered.

He suggested that McManus and the woman cop, who were both about the same size, trade clothes. "He'll never I.D. you for a cop," Rothmiller said. "Just go on up there and act like a friend. Try it."

Rothmiller's colleague thought about it awhile and decided it was just crazy enough to work. Amid hoots and catcalls from everyone in the station, the two cops arranged a private exchange of garments. Naturally the chiding became even more intense when the male cop emerged in the woman's getup looking like a third-rate Liza Minnelli act.

McManus endured the jeering and drove over to

the man's address in his glittery outfit. Then this cop working within the confines of one of the most homophobic institutions in the world made a bit of division history.

"Jimmy doesn't live here," the resident told him. He acted like he might like to continue the conversation, though, and McManus asked himself in. The resident, attired only in boxer shorts, sat on the sofa and made a quick pass at the demure, haltered cop. But during the harmless comedy of manners that followed, McManus did secure the information he was after, and not long afterward he would find his man.

Returning to the station house, McManus told his story, laughing at himself all the while. It became a great joke around the division. But to Rothmiller, his friend, and some others, it was also a valuable lesson: a cop didn't have to look for information holding a notepad and dressed in a nondescript suit, black shoes, and white socks. He could instead try to blend in with his surroundings and use his head. This required no false reports or perjury or other illegal tricks, just a little imagination and the courage to act a part.

There were some excellent detectives in the division, but not many of these veterans were willing to surrender their identity as a cop even for a few minutes, and this unwillingness to try different tactics pared down their flow of information. Rothmiller, while laughing at his friend's antics along with the others, also figured he'd made a gutsy play, completed an excellent chess move.

And by braving the taunts and playing the role of a cross dresser, McManus had demonstrated that he was absolutely comfortable with his own sexual identity. He could play a role, still be himself, and do valuable work on a case.

While on loan to Hollywood vice, Rothmiller had to pay his dues along with everyone else, busting streetwalkers. The never-ending fight to keep some sort of lid on open prostitution and all the other crimes it generated led to an elaborate verbal dance between cops and hookers.

The whores were out to weed out the cops from the johns. And the cops, in order to make a clean bust, had to get the hookers to suggest that sex be traded for money. If the cop mentioned money before she did, this constituted entrapment, and the arrest would not hold up in court.

Lots of cops, tired of jousting with well-coached whores, just offered money first, then made the bust and lied about it later. It was one of the many little perjuries cops learned to commit in order to make their jobs easier.

Rothmiller attacked the problem differently. He saw it more like a game than a chore, and he wanted to win cleanly. So he had business cards printed that described him as a vice president of locations for International Production Artist, with a home office in London. It was just the sort of murky but legitimate occupation likely to impress a hooker. And then came the barb on the hook. The card also described him as a nondeaf mute.

Looking like the amiable, easygoing fellow that he is, Rothmiller would drive up to a hooker in a new Cadillac provided by a cooperative auto dealer, smile, hand her his card, and listen to her bury herself. It was like making a good arrest and a harmless joke at the same time. A winning game.

When he took the woman around the corner to his waiting partner, he would begin to speak. "Must be a miracle!" one of the hookers exclaimed. "That's right," he said. "And you know what else? You're under arrest."

Most of the hookers took it well. An occasional bust came with the territory. Some of them continued laughing even as the handcuffs went on and they were hauled off to jail.

When the nondeaf-mute prosecutions started reaching the courts, the judges were elated. For once they could convict solicitors without suspecting they were in fact winking at perjured testimony. And they could share the joke.

Other cops detailed to vice started using the same tactic. And it worked for them too, because, as Rothmiller, a dedicated scuba diver, was to explain later, Hollywood hookers were like schools of fish. When you scattered them, others returned. And their communications with each other were not first-rate because they peddled their wares in a migrating cycle, moving from Hollywood to Anaheim (around Disneyland) to Inglewood (around the Great Western Forum, home of the Lakers) and back to Hollywood. The circuit usually took about a year. Meanwhile, the joke lasted.

But then a lieutenant stepped in. "Cut it out," he told Rothmiller.

Why? Rothmiller asked him.

"Because it's undignified," the lieutenant said.

Rothmiller was tempted to ask why if it was undignified for cops to hand out the mute cards, it was somehow dignified for women officers to cruise Sunset Boulevard in paint and miniskirts in order to bust johns. But he knew better than to ask. He knew degrading women officers was accepted because the LAPD brass didn't view them as real officers anyway.

Part of the problem in undercover work was that in order to succeed, the cop-actor had to ingratiate himself with others in order to arrest them. You befriended people, then you took them down. This required a strong sense of purpose. An occasional close call that put Rothmiller in jeopardy of a group beating or worse helped to keep things in perspective.

There was also a pronounced tendency among

general citizens and the judiciary itself to wink at bookmaking as a fact of life—a victimless crime. But bookies were often tied in to other nasty dealings such as extortion, loan sharking, and dealing in drugs and hot merchandise. One thing led to another; a bookmaker appeared somewhat more menacing when slapping around a terrified elderly woman or ripping off her wedding ring to secure his payoff.

A couple of homicide detectives, a pair generally regarded as untrustworthy, once tipped Rothmiller's identity to a bookmaker he and his partner, Pete Acuna, had been "operating" (setting up for a bust). Rothmiller broke the code of silence after he and his partner's lives had been put in jeopardy by these two fuck-ups. Nothing was proven in a court of law, but circumstantial evidence was solid. The pogue reaction was typically nonsensical. The cops who blew Rothmiller's cover received a slap on the wrist; they were suspended for ten days, charged with drinking on the job, so their more serious transgressions didn't soil their record.

Once Acuna went into a tough Hispanic bar in El Sereno to operate it for bookmaking. He'd been there before. The only way to bust such an operation was to chip away at it a day at a time, earning trust along the way.

While Rothmiller waited on a nearby bluff as backup, Acuna, a polished undercover man, remained inside a good three to four hours. He was supposed to be out in an hour, and as each minute went past, Rothmiller didn't know whether to call for backup or go in himself—which could jeopardize the play—or continue waiting.

Cops had a danger signal for these situations. If anything went wrong, the cop inside was supposed to break a window, using a bullet if he had to.

Acuna had made no signal, and Rothmiller heard no sounds of violence, so he relied on Acuna's undercover skills. He kept waiting.

But it was a nervous wait. Finally Acuna emerged with a group of men, their arms around each other. They were all drunk as lords.

It turned out that Acuna had been put through a special wringer. He was forced to down shooters with the other men, who questioned him repeatedly: "Are you a fucking cop or what?" But Acuna held his own, and fortunately his interrogators stayed with him drink for drink. Ultimately he passed the test. Rothmiller and Acuna took them all down a few days later.

About this time Rothmiller was effecting and perfecting his undercover role of Mike Lange, a standard Hollywood sleazeball in clanging jewelry and loud shirt who'd fricassee his grandmother for a price. In the underworld, he was a guy you could trust. He often carried business cards listing himself as a "consultant."

Rothmiller learned that if he went undercover in just the right situation, he could accomplish more police work in two hours than he could in days asking questions as a cop. Rothmiller didn't particularly enjoy playing his sleazeball role, but he did enjoy the results it achieved and he didn't feel it confused his own identity. Like his friend's borrowed halter top, it was just a device.

Rothmiller in his Lange persona drifted in and out of scumbag bars, race tracks, card rooms, and greasy all-night diners, always looking for a sure thing or a new angle. Like other lowlifes on the prowl, Lange lived high when he had a good scam working, and sometimes he frequented the Polo Lounge or other upscale joints around Beverly Hills and the West Side.

* * *

The jail in the Northeast Station had been condemned after the big 1971 quake, so cops took most of their suspects to Parker Center to be booked. But there were a few usable holding cells. One night a low-level crook was taken into a holding cell there before getting booked for an old traffic warrant.

Naturally the cops were taking their own sweet time. While he waited, the prisoner saw some other cops drag in a guy in handcuffs and slam him into the same cell. "Get in there, you motherfucker!"

"Motherfuck you, you cop asshole!" the second prisoner yelled.

He was a white man with a nasty attitude and a lot of jewelry that might or might not be fake.

"What are you in for?" the first prisoner asked him after a while.

"I don't know. Who the fuck knows around here? Nothin'! I didn't do nothin', goddammit! They're complete assholes."

A standard lowlife answer. Lowlifes never did anything. They just got angry when they were caught.

After a while the cops came back to take the second prisoner somewhere and they pretty much repeated the first exchange. But this time the cops slammed him around a little harder and he did what he could for a guy in handcuffs.

About a week later the first prisoner sat in a scumbag bar when in walked the standup guy from the Northeast lockup who'd been thrown into his cell. The guy sat down next to him but didn't seem to recognize him.

"Hey, how you doing, buddy?"

"Who the fuck are you?" the second man said.

"Don't you remember? We were cellmates?"

Big smile. "Well I'll be damned! How you doing?"

"Better. What's your name, pal?"

"Mike Lange. What's yours?"

And now Rothmiller was instantly accepted at a bar he wanted to operate—a bar he happened to know this sleazeball liked to hang out in. Rothmiller as Lange was now in perfect position to penetrate whatever was going on in this particular corner of the underworld—stolen swag, drugs, gambling, unlicensed firearms, burglaries, heists, smuggling stolen vehicles. Crooks didn't always specialize. They hitched up to whatever they thought might work and they often worked several scams at once.

L.A., like any big American city, was teeming in its nether corners with rackets big and small, connected like an ever-changing web in an altering pattern of cons and conspiracies.

But of course undercover operators and informants trying to deposit favors in the police bank were a constant hazard to these racketeers, absolute trust a rare commodity. It all varied from day to day, deal to deal.

The big test came the day Rothmiller as Lange was operating a bar and someone casually stuck a gun in his gut.

"You're a fucking cop," the voice said. Rothmiller didn't focus on the face. Just the gun. But he heard the voice. It was low and serious and Rothmiller had about thirty seconds to change it to a chuckle, convince this guy his doubts were insane.

He couldn't possibly know at this point whether this slimeball had solid information or was just making a periodic check of an acquaintance. But it all fell on Rothmiller. He had to be totally convincing without giving off any body language that showed fear or betrayal. It was Oscar time. No retakes, no method acting courses to fall back on.

And when he walked away with his life and his shift was over, he was supposed to go home and forget about it. Just another day at the office.

Working undercover, a cop could turn over cases he had never expected to work on. It was like surveillance. Rothmiller never knew where it might lead. If he was going after a bookie and he turned over a burglary along the way, he didn't ignore the find.

But Rothmiller also enjoyed the idea of going after criminals the way they went after society—on several fronts at once. Specialization had its advantages, but so did being a generalist in the war against crime. Later on, when he would enter the Organized Crime Intelligence Division, his capacity to shift gears and change identities would become a trademark. Of course he didn't think about it during his days in vice, but working undercover was precisely what secret police had been doing for centuries.

But because he was on the LAPD, Rothmiller was an undercover cop working for LAPD pogues, and that didn't make the job any easier.

"Pogue" is LAPD jargon for a supervisor who is worthless on the street but who can share the secret handshake of bureaucratic mediocrity with the other pogues. He will pass his oral promotion tests, which are of course administered by other pogues in the cyclical process that enables old pogues to beget new pogues.

After the Rodney King beating, Mayor Bradley appointed former Deputy Secretary of State Warren Christopher to head a seven-member commission to find out what was wrong with the LAPD. Among the Christopher Commission's findings: The department places undue reliance on oral sections of promotion tests. In other words, the LAPD too often promotes the wrong people:

pogues. This was not exactly new information to the real cops in the department.

A cop who wanted to do his job and stay out of hot water had to do it in such a way as not to alienate the pogues. And there were times these two goals—good police work, massaging the pogues—ran at cross purposes.

Once Rothmiller and his partner Acuna twisted information from an Archie Bunker type they had pulled in on a lewd conduct charge. They played good cop–bad cop on him and it worked like a charm, Acuna threatened to throw the book at Archie. Rothmiller said maybe they could go easy if he would help them. They could even arrange to reduce his charge to trespassing—a good deal for everybody.

Posing as Mike Lange and Pete Lima, carpet cleaners with names on their work shirts, they entered a bar on Verdugo Road with their informant, Archie, who promised them there was heavy bookmaking action behind the bar. There was, but this was one of those neighborhood places where everyone knew everyone, and it would take a great deal of time to get inside the operation. The two vice cops decided it would be worth it, and they worked the bar steadily after that, stopping in, buying drinks, doing their best to be accepted.

They even went to the bar's Christmas party on their day off rather than offend anybody. They were so intent on taking down this bar, they decided that if anyone tried to hire them as carpet cleaners, they would rent equipment and go out and clean the carpets. They would not be deterred.

After about three months they were almost ready to close in. One day a new supervisor transferred in—a sergeant who'd never worked vice. Much of his experience had been in the Internal Affairs division. Rothmiller and Acuna were showing him the ropes one night, and they explained that as part of their rounds they would spend a couple of hours in the bar on Verdugo. They told him they would leave the place about 9 P.M., and they repeated the universal signal for vice cops in trouble—a broken window.

Inside the bar, patrons were telling story after story, and the two cops were having trouble getting away politely, so they were still inside at 9:15 when suddenly their raw vice sergeant came crashing in with a squad of uniforms. He went right up to Rothmiller and Acuna: "Mike, Pete, are you guys okay?"

Every patron in the bar turned to the carpet-cleaning duo. "You guys are *cops?*"

Three months of work finished. Acuna leapt from his barstool and grabbed the pogue around the neck, choking him. The two men rolled out in the street, stopping traffic, as the other cops tried to pull Acuna off. Meanwhile, all the patrons took off.

"You dumb motherfucker!" Acuna screamed. "You stupid motherfucking pogue son of a bitch!"

"Pete, Pete, you want to make sergeant!" the other cops yelled, trying to pry him off. They finally managed to, but as he looked over and saw the face of the gasping pogue, Acuna leapt on him again. "You stupid son of a bitch! Three months of work down the drain!"

Eventually, the other cops pulled Acuna away again, and when they all got back to the station, the sergeant declared he would report this whole affair to the Internal Affairs Division. Rothmiller helped to mediate the situation.

Yes, Rothmiller conceded, the sergeant was only trying to help, but if he was worried, all he had to do was stop in the bar and buy a drink or even send patrolmen in on a pretext. He didn't have to blow his cops' cover.

"But he put his hands on me!" the sergeant protested.

True, and that was awful. But if a report were filed, the sergeant's actions would not look terribly astute either. Why not just forget the whole thing?

Which eventually they all said they would do. But no one really forgot it. It made one hell of a pogue story.

One day, after years of ruling his desk domain, yet another vice sergeant decided to flex his muscles and take a quick fling undercover. He no doubt wanted to prove he was one of the guys, that his prowess as a cop did not stop at the station door.

"Let's go after a fruit," he said.

Rothmiller and his partner didn't particularly favor this part of their work, but as vice cops they were called upon from time to time to make some lewd conduct cases. Most citizens probably assumed that in this era of sexual freedom, cops were no longer detailed to trap homosexuals. But unfortunately, a sizeable number of gays still insisted on performing their trysts in public places, which made it unlawful. Only the very real threat of a bust seemed to dampen their enthusiasm for open relations.

So while serious crimes continued tearing at the fabric of society, LAPD cops were still employed to go out and arrest gay lawbreakers.

It was a warm Saturday afternoon, and the sun was bursting through the inner-city smog like beams of chemical fire. The pogue sergeant accompanied the two plainclothes officers to one of the many parks in Los Angeles frequented by gays. The park they chose was a relatively short hop north along the freeway from the glass-and-steel towers of downtown L.A. It was bordered on one side by the Pasadena Freeway and on the other by Figueroa

Street—a sycamore-lined greenbelt that had as its centerpiece a fortress-like concrete structure housing the public rest rooms.

The cops parked their gray four-door Plymouth sedan on a service road about 100 yards from the building. Although the vehicle was partially hidden by shrubs and trees, anyone in the park who saw it would spot them as cops. In minority neighborhoods like this one, even the youngest child could easily identify unmarked police cars.

But Rothmiller and his partner didn't care. It only made the job more challenging. And this way anyone they arrested was more likely to be a flagrant offender.

The sergeant, eager to be the point man for this expedition, paced in front of the rest room building while Rothmiller and his partner settled back for the wait. They watched him start a conversation with a young Hispanic boy about eleven years old. After talking for quite a long time, the sergeant and the kid both moved out of sight toward the bathroom entrance.

Not much later, their supervisor came running toward them with all afterburners on. He was clearly panicked, looked like he was being chased by Bela Lugosi on a bicycle. Arms and knees pumping, he started screaming: "Go, go, go! Start the car! Go!"

When he got to within about 40 yards of the car, they saw a group of Hispanic men, perhaps a dozen of them, charging around the corner at full tilt, screaming less than complimentary words at the fleeing pogue. "Motherfucker! You son of a bitch!"

Rothmiller and his partner could size up the situation all right, but they hadn't yet figured out what caused it. Now the sergeant yelled, "Start the car! Start the car! Open the door! Open the door!"

Rothmiller whipped the vehicle around and his partner opened the door. The sergeant, sucking air like a racehorse, desperately lunged headlong into the rear seat. Rothmiller floored the Plymouth, slinging gravel, then careened through picnic tables and sunbathers.

The car pulled away from the still-screaming group of Hispanics, flew over the curb, and disappeared up Figueroa.

"What's going on?" Rothmiller yelled.

"Ah shit! Oh God, they were going to kill me!" he answered, heaving uncontrollably, his face crimson. "Jesus!"

"What do you mean? What happened?" Rothmiller's partner said.

"The kid . . . that kid. I was convinced he . . . he was hustling. I thought he was a prostitute!"

"A prostitute!" Rothmiller said, laughing now. "He was only about ten or twelve years old. What made you think he was a prostitute?"

"Well, I saw him sitting on the guardrail outside the men's room. I said, 'Hi,' and he said 'Hi' back to me."

It was difficult to even follow this ridiculous pogue's reasoning. Because they were looking for prostitutes and lewd-conduct violations, he seemed to think they were everywhere you turned. But to this inner-city youngster, a guardrail was just a makeshift monkey bar. And a public rest room was no more than a rest room. The pogue, now outside his beloved station house, was up against reality, not his own preconceptions of life in this section of the city he was supposed to police with some understanding.

The sergeant had been frustrated by the youngster's unwillingness to bite on any of the police word games to trap prostitutes and public sex freaks. Taking an approach commonly used by bungling cops, the supervisor simply broke the law. He lured him to the rest room, drew out twenty dollars, and said, "Would you suck my dick?"

The kid ran, screamed for help, and the rest made public park history.

A close call like that would make most people pause for some critical self-analysis or maybe even try staying within the limits of the law. But this sergeant wanted to plunge back in without asking any questions about just where he might have gone wrong. It was typical pogue behavior not to admit to any lack of knowledge.

Nevertheless, Rothmiller and his partner, hoping to avoid another near homicide, race riot, or high-speed chase, gave him a Cliff Notes version of how to operate in this particular arena of police work.

A few days later they rendezvoused with their sergeant at another park a little farther up the freeway. Rothmiller told the sergeant that roughly 80 percent of the men's room clientele were gay men looking for quick sex. Later, the two cops realized it was a mistake telling him what the percentages were likely to be. In any case, there was no going back. The sergeant was in charge.

This park was a pleasant oasis in the heart of L.A., with great stands of magnificent elm and oak. The rest rooms were in a low-key stucco building in a grassy, shaded area. The three cops sat on a bench, Rothmiller and his partner tactfully repeating the mini-lesson on how to handle any conversations. They also told their supervisor what to look for in a suspect: someone who drove in very slowly, looked all around him, then parked his car and sat for several minutes with his head on a swivel. When he got out, he would stand in front of the car a minute or so, then meander toward the rest room, probably stopping several times as he scanned the park.

A few minutes later the first men's room patron came down the chute. But he drove up with no hesitation, stepped out, and walked directly to the men's room.

"I don't think so," Rothmiller said.

"Why not?" asked the supervisor-pupil.

"Because he just went straight into the head. Let's wait for the next one."

But the sergeant was already up and moving. "No, no, no . . . I'll see what's up."

The sergeant had been in the men's room less than a minute when he stepped out of the doorway and gave the high sign—a hand brushed through his hair.

On the bench, Rothmiller and his partner were caught off-guard. "Hey, he's got a violation," Rothmiller said.

As he and his partner approached the sergeant, the average-looking man in his late thirties emerged from the rest room. The sergeant flashed his badge and told him he was under arrest.

"Under arrest? For what?"

"Lewd conduct," the sergeant said.

The man immediately became frantic. The sergeant shook his head, ignored the protests, and went back in another car while Rothmiller and his partner cuffed the prisoner and read him his rights. On the way to the station, the arrested man sat aghast in the backseat, pleading his innocence over and over, hoping for leniency somehow from these two underlings of his tormenter. They tried to calm him down, but they'd heard it all before, from doctors, lawyers, working men, family men, a Midwestern police chief, even one priest.

Still, the suspect's actions were not typical. He was unusually adamant. He hadn't done a thing, he said. He just went in there and used the toilet. He couldn't understand what was happening to him, he said.

The sergeant's arrest report told a much different story. It said the man was seated on a toilet with an erect penis, that he was masturbating, and that he motioned to the sergeant to come over and take it in his mouth. The sergeant exited, gave the two partners the signal, and the arrest was made. It was a typical arrest for lewd conduct: quick, easy, nasty.

In the vice room at the Northeast Station, the man said over and over, "I just went in there to take a shit!" He was unusually vehement in his denial. Usually by the time they got to the station, even the most distressed suspects in these cases admitted their guilt, at the same time begging to be let off.

Eventually the suspect divulged his profession; he was a county social worker dealing with sexually abused children. Every cop in the room took a deep breath. This guy was fighting for his life. A conviction would spell the end of his career. And sure enough, the sergeant called the man's supervisor and notified her of the arrest.

Before the trial date, the defendant's supervisor wanted to find out more about the case. She said this would be a crucial part of the administrative investigation to determine whether or not the man would keep his job. The sergeant arranged a meeting with her.

"Listen," he told Rothmiller and his partner, "this lady is coming in and she wants to see the park. And, do your damnedest to arrest somebody," he demanded. "Arrest somebody in front of her so she'll know what this place is like."

They took her back to the same park, where they did not have to wait long. Within minutes, Rothmiller and his partner nailed two classic textbook violations, one after another. All of this was a surreal experience for the supervising social worker. The two cops had showed off a bit, telling her step by step what would happen before it happened: where the suspects would park their cars, how they would approach the men's room.

Just for the woman's benefit, the cops sat the two men down on different benches, advised them of their rights, and interviewed them right in the park.

Both men freely admitted to the charges of lewd conduct and were happy to volunteer just why they loved this particular park.

Clearly what she had seen influenced what she thought of her employee. "You guys were right," she said. "We would never have guessed. We would never have known." At this point Rothmiller was bothered by the automatic assumption that because this man had been looking for men's room sex, he would be a danger to children. He and his partner had both dealt enough in this arena to know that in a vast majority of cases this would be a ridiculous assumption.

The man fought the charge all the way, but a few months later the sergeant testified in court and got his conviction. Now he was a former social worker and a registered sex offender. His life as he knew it was destroyed.

A short time later, the case came up in conversation.

"Do you remember that social worker I popped for lewd conduct?" the sergeant said.

"Yes?"

"I lied. The guy didn't actually do anything. He was just taking a shit. But he was in there, so he must be a fruit, so I figured what the hell."

It was one of those instances when the truth seemed so logical, Rothmiller and his partner were disgusted with themselves for not seeing it. From start to finish, here was a man who showed only innocence. It was all clear now.

Yet the sergeant seemed proud of having taken this noncase completely through the process, from making the arrest all the way to conviction, somehow ignoring the tragedy he had created for another human being. Just as he had convinced himself the man was guilty without witnessing a violation, he could now convince himself he was a smooth undercover cop—an operator. Why didn't Rothmiller do something to stop this travesty? Why did he ignore the signs pointing toward innocence? And why did he continue to keep quiet after being flatly informed that his supervisor had lied? And not only lied, he had perjured himself to convict an innocent person.

But you didn't question a fellow officer. You backed him up. You worried about it later. If the cop proved to be a jerk, you might tell him so to his face. But you continued to back him up; that was the brotherhood of law enforcement.

This rule of the street governed every facet of life as a police officer. Beyond conscious thought, it developed into a reflex, like pulling your hand from a flame. There was no alternative action to consider. You backed up your fellow officers. Any other course was suicidal.

This pogue sergeant was Rothmiller's supervisor at the time, the person who wrote his rating reports. In a specialized unit like vice, a supervisor had even greater powers over his subordinates.

Vice was an eighteen-month gig, unless an officer was promoted while in the unit. Generally, an officer did his time, learned the ropes, then left before every potential offender in the city memorized his face. But if an officer was thrown out before his time was up, he was dead meat. His career was over.

Turning on his supervisor gave a cop the worst possible jacket in all of law enforcement because every supervisor in the department would then have everything to fear and nothing to gain from having him around. To them, he would be the lowest form of animal life—a cop who couldn't be trusted to uphold the first commandment of law enforcement. And he not only snitched, he snitched up, not down, trying to mount a case against his own supervisor.

With this type of jacket, six months would be an optimistic assessment of a cop's future with the department. Even the most mentally tough individual could not withstand the unrelenting campaign of terror that would be undertaken against him. He would be a target for supervisors and fellow officers alike, a fink despised by all and on everybody's trouble list. Without question, his life as a policeman would change almost as dramatically as the life of that poor man who took a dump in the wrong men's room.

If a cop actually did go about trying to turn in a negative report against his own supervisor, he'd be expected to go up the chain of command a notch or two to a lieutenant or captain. Said potentate would listen to the story, then confront the supervisor with the charges. Of course the supervisor would deny them and immediately question the motives of the reporting officer. Why would he make such wild accusations?

In Rothmiller's supervisor's case, the cop had made the arrest and written out the report, all under oath. So either he lied at the time or later. In the end, it would just have been Rothmiller's word against the word of his superior.

In misconduct cases there was always the Internal Affairs Division to turn to. They were the people trained to handle these matters. Trouble was, reality tended to step in. Supervisors always won. Period. Especially when there was no irrefutable evidence of misconduct. Most likely, the department would just turn the tables by using a common tactic of accusing the accuser. Now the poor cop trying to right a wrong would be charged with making false and misleading statements and with conduct unbecoming an officer.

At about this point the cop could possibly ask the defense attorney to petition the court to reopen the case and allow the introduction of new evidence. A long shot at best. Even if the pogue himself decided to recant his testimony, the odds of the court accepting a new version would still be slim. In most cases, courts viewed recanted testimony as unreliable and were often suspicious of the motives for a belated change of heart.

Fact is, challenging another officer, particularly a superior officer, remained a losing proposition. Had Rothmiller been willing to sacrifice his career to try to amend the sergeant's wrong, the result would no doubt be unchanged. The man in the rest room would remain a sex offender, the supervisor would still be in a position of power, and the police department would still be run the same way.

And so cops, even the most straight-ahead cops, were sometimes party to the injustices frequently perpetrated on innocent people by the worst officers. With cops floating each day in a tossing sea of false reports and perjury, somebody innocent would occasionally go down. It was inevitable. But because everyone in the department supported the situation as it had evolved, the system was as powerful as the tides. For a cop to stand in its way was inviting the cold blackness of the sea to close over him.

Still, it was this particular case of the screwed, singled-out social worker that made Rothmiller see the terrible dangers inherent in a system of law that had been twisted and based on false statements made by a corps of individual vigilantes on the public payroll. It was kangaroo justice. Even if its intentions had originally been benign, the result was anything but.

Every day veteran officers taught the subtleties of circumventing the laws to their younger officers. And when the tricks didn't work, the veterans said, falsify the arrest reports. Decide who is guilty and then construct a report that made it so. Often these tactics put deserving individuals behind bars. Other times they were used simply as retribution for some wrong perceived by the cop. Just as commonly, they were used by supervisors looking for gold stars in their personnel files.

Because pogues knew how to impress other pogues, these fantasy files made many undeserving bureaucrats look like supercops on paper. And in this case, the records showed, a canny supervisor went out on the street and proved he could pop an offender in minutes, take him all the way to court, and win. What a stud.

Years later this same supervisor had another story to tell Rothmiller. This one involved no perjury or unlawful prosecution. It was all perfectly legal.

The sergeant, who had children, always had a live-in housekeeper to keep things running at home. He found these women through a downtown agency clearly not interested in whether its domestic workers were documented or not. It was a good way to find people who would work for lower wages.

This particular sergeant could never seem to keep a housekeeper with him more than a few months. One day, when his domestic help situation came up in a conversation, he told Rothmiller he needed to find a new employee right away.

"That last one I had wasn't working out too well," he said, "and I owed her three months' wages, so I took her down to INS and turned her in."

The Immigration and Naturalization Service offices were in the Federal Building, across the street from police headquarters at Parker Center, so, as it turned out, he had run his errand while he had to stop in at headquarters anyway. It was like stopping off for a loaf of bread at a convenience store. This legal act of betrayal had in essence provided him with a slave for three months. She'd taken care of his children and his home and received nothing in return for her work. and was betrayed and discarded like a piece of garbage.

Not long afterward, the sergeant was promoted.

· 5 ·

Mickey Tells a Story

A reporter for KABC TV, Wayne Satz, was creating a King Kong–sized furor around town by interviewing an LAPD cop known within the department as the Masked Marvel. The Masked Marvel, who appeared on camera over a series of six nightly newscasts, was educating L.A. viewers about his employer. He did this while wearing a scuba diver's hood. Technicians distorted his voice.

The Masked Marvel felt the need to conceal his identity because some of the stories he told were about citizens being beaten, choked, humiliated, and otherwise abused by Los Angeles police officers without provocation or legal justification. He also said LAPD cops were "extremely eager" to shoot somebody and that most of them were racial bigots. Additionally, he complained that the LAPD brass at best looked the other way, at worst encouraged the street justice being meted out day after day.

Of course for years many people had been complaining about exactly the sort of abuse the Masked

Marvel described, but most of them were dismissed as "people of color" or "bleeding-heart ACLU liberals." Now the Marvel was supporting this line of thought from, of all places, inside the LAPD.

This made the department, from top to bottom, less than happy with both the Marvel and Wayne Satz. Just about all hands on the LAPD pulled the wagons in a circle and prayed for the quick demise of these two video tormenters who night after night chipped away at them like a pair of zealous golfers playing under the lights.

Thou shalt not fink on another cop, aghast cops said. This public transgression of the commandment was more than they could bear. Cops placed Satz's photo on their targets at the shooting range. The department even filed a libel suit against KABC, which a judge quickly threw out.

Meanwhile, the brass let it be known that they would do just about anything for the heroic cop who could crack this case and identify the rat fink in the diver's hood. Anything to put an end to this news show nightmare. Solving murders and all that other stuff was okay, but the big case was the case of Wayne Satz and his Masked Marvel from Hell.

The LAPD launched what was probably the biggest manhunt in its history to learn the identity of the Masked Marvel. Cops from top to bottom were told to report anything they could think of that might bring him in. Proof? Not necessary. Suspicion was more than adequate. A clue, an untoward thought, a murmer, a glance, anything. Just tell Blue Brother, who would take it from there.

At one point, when KABC showed the Masked Marvel in his police uniform with the badge number taped, the camera closed in on the Marvel's hands. The LAPD made a still shot from the videotape and blew it up into a poster, examining the hands in detail for telltale scars or marks or configurations.

Word circulated around the department that cops were being detailed to tail Satz in an effort to discover his damnable informant. At this time Rothmiller was assigned to the Northeast division on loan to the Hollywood Prostitution Task Force. One night, driving past Griffith Park with his partner, Rothmiller thought he spotted Satz at the wheel of a Fiat sports car. To satisfy his curiosity, he checked the license plate over the radio, and sure enough, it was Satz.

That was really the end of it. Rothmiller and his partner, Pete Acuna, stopped following as soon as the plate was verified—a matter of a few blocks. But when they ran the plate on an open frequency, word got out around the department that Rothmiller and Acuna were on his tail. Then the rumor became more expansive. Not long afterward, it was said that the two vice cops had pulled Satz over and worked him over. Other cops were coming up to them and congratulating them for a job well done.

"No," Rothmiller said, "maybe someone is following Satz around, but it's not me and Pete. We never even talked to the guy."

Cops would wink at the denial. "Yeah, sure, we understand." So the vice duo became heroes for a beating they didn't commit. This was a path to respect in the LAPD: get everyone to believe you'd assaulted a reporter for broadcasting the truth.

Eventually, a year or so after the series ran, the Masked Marvel quit the force and unmasked himself. He turned out to be John Mitchell, one of the brighter officers who'd graduated with Rothmiller in his police academy class of 1972.

The Masked Marvel series had appeared five years after the two cadets' class hit the streets as rookies. Rothmiller was intrigued by the fact that one of his own classmates—someone who'd become a cop at the same time he did—was already so disgusted with the pattern of abuse by the LAPD that he would resort to such a circus tactic. Clearly, on this job, burnout could come early.

Rothmiller remembered Mitchell as a sensitive young man who had been a mortician before he joined the police force. A few years after the unmasking, the two men ran into each other at a gym in Fountain Valley, and they talked over old times at the LAPD. Mitchell was happy to see that Rothmiller still warmed to him and, unlike so many LAPD cops, bore him no ill will over the Masked Marvel episode.

Mitchell struck Rothmiller as the kind of cop who had a genuine liking for the citizens he met out on patrol. The violence and cruelty he witnessed nightly on the streets of Los Angeles had failed to make him callous. Instead he was genuinely pained for the too often brutal responses he saw from cops who had become prematurely cynical out on the job.

Rothmiller didn't always have to play an elaborate ruse to take down criminals. Sometimes the key was just getting somebody to give him the right information. Working informants was always at the core of plainclothes work. Cops and crooks trading favors, a time-honored practice with enough twists and turns to confuse a pretzel maker.

Lots of criminals were more than willing to turn in someone else in an effort to improve their own situations. Lots of others were happy to provide false information if they could find cops naive enough to buy their stories. So cops used informants to check tales of other informants without informing them just who else fit into their information network. This further complicated these tenuous situations. Some informants were tough customers who provided information only after cops had "squeezed" them like oranges. There were lots of ways to squeeze an informant.

Not many of these snitches were rolling bandages for the Red Cross in their spare time. Virtually all of them worked schemes of their own that they tried to protect while helping cops corral someone else. Mostly, informants wanted their enemies busted. Their enemies were, in many cases, competitors working the same criminal scheme.

Later on in his career, after Rothmiller was working as an intelligence detective, he began sharing one of his informants with a U.S. Drug Enforcement agent. This was a common practice, too. Cops from different agencies traded favors just like cops and informants did. After Rothmiller turned his informant over to the DEA, he didn't have reason to contact him for a while, and the DEA pretty much took over the man's favors.

But one day Rothmiller arranged to meet the DEA agent at the informant's home in El Toro. When Rothmiller walked in, he found the informant in the living room with at least a pound of cocaine on the glass coffee table. He was dividing it into sale packages while the DEA man calmly sat looking on. Nowadays the biggest dealers are moving cocaine in one-hundred-pound lots or more. But in the early eighties, a pound of cocaine was a major score for any cop.

The informant was just finishing up. He scooped up all the residue in his fingers. "I don't do drugs," he said with a smile, "but I can't stand to let this stuff go to waste." Then he licked his fingers.

Rothmiller, who didn't like the looks of this at all, motioned the agent into another room. "What's going on here?" he said.

The federal agent explained that his informant was helping him take down some other dealers and that he also claimed to have information on a major hydroponic marijuana-growing operation in Colorado. "You gotta do what you gotta do." The agent shrugged in apology.

It was a common practice. A cop buddied up with a crook and took out his enemies for him. The cop earned lots of arrests; the crook had a clear ticket to financial success and, at least for a while, a life free of prosecution. There was often a degree of personal chemistry involved in these cop-informant relationships, a meeting of the minds that the cops didn't want to think about.

In this particular situation, a drug dealer of relative importance was no doubt helping to bust smaller compretititors while promising to bring in somebody bigger down the road. A deal with the devil to scoop up some little demons. Meanwhile, the DEA agent scored lots of good arrests. It wasn't always so easy to know where to draw the line. This didn't appear to be one of those times. The DEA agent had been conned by the dealer and conned by his own wandering values.

The dynamics of informing were like that, not a pretty process. Rothmiller had once busted a book-maker after a supposedly reputable lawyer "dropped a dime" on him. The bookie had been the lawyer's own client. This wasn't all that uncommon. A criminal lawyer who couldn't handle his BMW payment might be sorely tempted to set the wheels of justice turning.

The client would never know who turned him in. He spent perhaps a couple of hours in jail, and then the lawyer demanded $15,000 up front to take the case. Presto, the lawyer's creditors were gone for a while, justice was served, and the attorney-client relationship went on as before, with the bookie operating from a new location.

Sometimes detectives themselves dropped a dime on crooks. Only instead of calling police, they'd call a wife. Rothmiller first saw this one pulled by detectives in the Northeast division. They were after a criminal who was too smart to be caught. The only thing they caught him at was having an affair. So they informed his wife. A woman did the calling. It worked better that way.

Sometimes the cops would manufacture physical evidence first. "I hate to be the one to tell you this, but I think you better check the backseat of your husband's car." There a wife might discover women's undergarments, not her own, or perhaps a used condom.

Why put a strain on this individual's marriage? First, it was revenge. This guy was blatantly pulling capers on their turf, an arguable case for contempt of cop. Second, by causing him trouble at home, the cops threw a wrench into his operations, taking his energies away from his criminal activities. Later, when Rothmiller was promoted into OCID, he learned this was a standard practice among detectives from that division, Administrative Narcotics, the FBI, and detectives all over the country who were chasing big, smart crooks.

A variation of this method was like the buzzard who got tired of waiting; he went out and killed something. Detectives would lure the sucker into a trap with a call girl. This made it easier to get photographic evidence to squeeze the guy and perhaps get him to inform on somebody else. Lots of crooks who were experts at avoiding arrest for their racketeering activities were nevertheless easily disarmed by the right woman. And lots of cops had a list of call girls with whom they traded information and other favors.

There was an unmistakable element of glee when cops played with their enemies' personal relationships. It had the aspect of a practical joke. The cops would have a good laugh over these tactics.

And of course once the line had been crossed, it

was easy to manufacture adulterous "evidence" against marriages in which there was no hanky-panky at all. There were also cops who would use these tricks not against suspected criminals but against their perceived enemies. Not even J. Edgar Hoover thought Martin Luther King, Jr., was a dangerous criminal. He tried to squeeze King over his marital infidelities purely because Hoover personally disliked King and his cause.

Naturally, a cop who was just getting into the business might wonder about questions of moral legitimacy, but when these practices were accepted by the group, they were easier to swallow. Anyone who objected was the freak. Once again, it was only a short hop from the street justice meted out by patrol officers to the more sophisticated extralegal tricks of the detectives.

Another time-honored practice was to "stiff a call" against a mark. In these cases detectives wanted to go into closed premises somewhere—perhaps the headquarters of a suspected drug dealer—but they either didn't want to bother with a warrant or they didn't believe a judge would grant one. So they would call the police—that is, they would call themselves—with a tip that a serious crime was being committed at that address: a stabbing, a rape, something. Then cops would be radioed and would show up in force. Now if they happened to see anything, it was legally admissible evidence.

Crooks were on to this tactic, and of course they would try to block the cops from entering. "Bullshit, everything's okay here." But the cops would come in force, and as long as they had that call on the 911 tape, they were in the clear. "Sorry, we have to come in. My my, what have we here? Look at all this cocaine." (Or it might be betting slips, burglar tools, illegal firearms, or burglary swag.) Now it was evidence.

L.A. SECRET POLICE

Rothmiller learned how to create unwilling informants. There were many ways to do this, all of them nasty. One method was to threaten to hang a snitch jacket on someone. The individual might well decide that it was healthier to be informing to the cops without everyone knowing about it than to refuse to turn informant and have all the wrong parties believe he was snitching anyway. In the underworld, just like everywhere else, perceptions could speak louder than realities.

If the cop's mark was arrested and booked into the L.A. County jail system waiting for his attorney to get him out, this opened another range of possibilities. There were holding tanks all over the county, and every day buses shifted prisoners from jail to jail within the vast system. A cop could put in a call and have his victim transferred from place to place with ease, losing him inside the system like a stone in a gravel pit. The jails' impossibly confusing telephone network aided the maneuver, acting as a barrier to lawyers and other outsiders. The Founding Fathers could never have foreseen this trick.

This routine not only made the victim's life miserable and kept him from his lawyers, it physically wore him out, making him susceptible to a cop "friend" who could ease his woes.

If this didn't work, he could be thrown in with whoever would make him scared or miserable: Black Muslims, Aryan Brotherhood, Mexican Mafia, you name it. Whoever they were, they could be found somewhere inside L.A.'s jail system.

An inmate was even more vulnerable to an unwarranted jacket than someone on the outside. He had no place to hide. And it was easy for cops to visit a prisoner, then loudly behave as though he were cooperating. An onslaught like this cracked some pretty tough nuts. Not pretty, but it worked.

Once informants became informants, they would

desperately seek protection from any possible retaliation. Cops were very free with their promises of protection. But if they actually protected all the informants who received their pledges, there would be no time for anything else. The informants wanted to believe the promises, though at a gut level many of them had to know they were being conned.

One day Rothmiller and his partner Acuna decided to look in on Patrick Pond. A well-known bookmaker and loan shark, Pond would lie low when there was heat, then jump back into business like a porpoise. He had an apartment south of the Cal State Los Angeles university campus. They watched him for a while, and sure enough, Pond was making rounds—checking phone spots for a bookmaking operation.

The two detectives decided to check with Administrative Vice, which was supposed to keep track of the bigger wheels in illegal L.A. gambling circles. They went to the detective who was reputed to be the biggest expert on bookmakers in the department, a premier vice detective. He even taught classes on vice at the police academy.

"What do you know about this guy Pond?" Rothmiller said. "We want to take him off. He's operating again."

Amazingly, both the expert and his partner said they had never heard of Pond, had nothing on one of the biggest bookies in the city! Either these two Ad Vice detectives were a lot dumber than their reputations would indicate or there was something rotten in Los Angeles.

Divisional vice cops took Sunday and Monday off. Everyone in Administrative Vice knew that. But Rothmiller and his partner went over to watch Pond's place on a Monday. Sure enough, the two detectives who said they'd never heard of Pond pulled up and walked straight into his apartment. They stayed inside about an hour, then emerged with Pond, who walked them to their car. They were all pals, joking together. The implication was clear.

Rothmiller and his partner reported what they'd learned to their sergeant. The sergeant, alarmed by their story, arranged for the three of them to meet with a command officer at the Winery, a downtown restaurant. There, surrounded by oak barrels of wine, Rothmiller and his partner told the story again.

They couldn't read anything one way or the other in the superpogue's eyes, but he told them to keep watching Pond. "Just keep after him. Let's see what he does next."

And the next day, yet another unit was called in—the mysterious Organized Crime Intelligence Division. Rothmiller, his partner, and their vice sergeant met with the OCID captain and two of his detectives, who wanted to know everything. This was Rothmiller's first brush with OCID. When the captain of Administrative Vice stepped in, it looked like the department was not going to ignore this.

But when Rothmiller and his partner returned to their surveillance of Pond, there was nothing left to see. Pond, who had been very active when they first started watching him, was no longer checking his phone spots. In fact, he was nowhere to be seen. They discovered his home phone was disconnected. He'd moved.

But Pond had his mail forwarded. They found his new address through the postal service. He wasn't far from the first place, living in a California-style apartment complex where all the doors led out onto a courtyard. Rothmiller and his partner sat within earshot of his new living room and heard enough of his bookie conversations to know they'd be able to get a search warrant and make a case against him.

But when they came to work the following day, they learned Pond had been murdered! He'd been bludgeoned to death in his apartment. Too many coincidences, though he had been a loan shark as well as a bookie, and loan sharks made lots of enemies. It was possible one of them had taken him out.

The two vice cops reported what they knew to the investigating homicide detectives. Homicide reported there had been no signs of a struggle. Two glasses of Coke were on the coffee table. Nothing appeared stolen or ransacked. It looked very much like Pond knew the person who killed him. No murder weapon was recovered.

But there was more: Patrol officers had been called to the scene by a suspicious neighbor. When they arrived and discovered the body, they found a cop was already there—a detective from Administrative Vice—the partner of the premier vice detective. That was the story Homicide gave Rothmiller. The homicide detectives said the vice cop was very nervous, said he was looking for something. He got out fast.

The dead bookie was about 5 feet, 5 inches and stout. But along with his own clothes was a stock of clothing for a man about the same size as the expert vice detective. The homicide detectives said another man had been staying with Pond. There was unspecified evidence of a homosexual relationship.

Suddenly the expert vice detective, who had more than twenty years' service, called in and said he was retiring immediately. Please send him the paperwork.

Sure. By the way, could he come in to headquarters? Some homicide detectives wanted to ask him about a case.

Sorry, can't make it, the premier detective said.

The retirement process could be handled a lot easier if he would come down and sign a few things, he was told.

No, he replied, mail them. Or talk to his attorney. But he wouldn't come down. Not for anything. Administrators then refused to mail his retirement identification. Retired policemen prize this I.D., which gives them a gun permit and essentially grants them immunity from traffic tickets for life. He'd have to come down for it, they said.

Forget it then, the cop said. Keep the stuff. He also left his wife. Rothmiller started asking whether the department would file murder charges. Homicide replied that the district attorney's office felt there was insufficient evidence: no murder weapon or prints. Neighbors at Pond's old apartment picked out photos of the two Administrative Vice detectives as people they had seen frequently around the apartment. But, Homicide told Rothmiller, the feeling was that the detectives would just tell a jury they were there investigating a criminal. Juries were not quick to convict cops of murder, especially celebrated detectives. Insufficient evidence.

As homicide detectives pieced it together for Rothmiller, the expert vice cop was having an affair with Pond. They believed he killed him for reasons unknown. The same cop had also given his lover thousands to put out on the street to earn loan-shark rates.

Homicide believed that the partner was innocent, probably wasn't even part of the rackets either. The premier vice detective, who had a forceful demeanor and the reputation of a man who knew what he was doing, had a habit of telling his partner to wait in the car while he checked things out.

So the partner was allowed to remain in the

department, although he was transferred elsewhere. No charges were filed and the case remained open.

Years later, one of the OCID detectives assigned to this sensitive case would reveal more details. There had been much dirty work to cover everything up, and some of it had been done by OCID. That's why the elite division was called in. Rothmiller and his partner had stumbled on a huge bookmaking operation, bigger than they suspected, perhaps the biggest in Southern California.

Pond had allegedly been paying off cops in Administrative Vice, including those high up in the department, probably all the way to the command officer they had met for lunch at the Winery. The celebrated vice detective had retrieved incriminating evidence of these payoffs just as the patrol officers arrived at the homicide scene. Homicide had misled Rothmiller on that point. The partner of the celebrated vice cop had been at the murder scene, and so had the celebrated vice cop.

When all this was pieced together by investigators at the time, the LAPD brass could not bear to see the image of the department so terribly tarnished. Over and over the LAPD had crowed over its reputation as the one major police department in America where nobody took cash in unmarked envelopes. There was stuff here just too awful to let outsiders see—a queer cop and cash bribes tied to a dead bookie with his head caved in. The department had to be protected. The murder was never solved, no one was charged with taking bribes, and life went on in the LAPD.

At the beginning of 1978, Rothmiller, on the prowl for information, was sitting in an east Los Angeles watering hole called Brandy's. With him were a couple of detectives he knew from OCID— the same men who'd been on the Pond case.

Brandy's was in the Hollenbeck division. Its customers were a curious mixture of legitimate citizens, sleazeballs, and cops. The sleazeballs here were the lowest of the low—a crew of criminals and outcasts who would have fit nicely in the famous *Star Wars* bar scene.

Rothmiller still didn't know much about OCID. But after working the Pond case, he ran into the OCID detectives again when they inexplicably decided to tag along on some arrests. They were always looking for information and not terribly willing to trade any back. But they occasionally would throw Rothmiller a bone for his own case file.

As the three cops spoke in low tones, Rothmiller looked across the bar and spotted a face he knew; actually it was a face most people would think they knew, because it was the face of Philip De Petro, a tiny little guy who looked enough like Mickey Rooney to be his twin. De Petro had two street monickers—one, of course, was Mickey Rooney. The other was Sleazy. He was a third-rate hoodlum who worked a variety of scams—fencing swag, bookmaking, whatever was quick or easy. He was always sticking his nose into things. He was the kind of guy John Gotti would have sent out for a pizza.

Rothmiller was pretty sure De Petro was wanted on a felony bookmaking warrant, but he wasn't totally sure. It didn't look like the little guy was going anywhere, so the three cops went down to the station to check outstanding warrants. Sure enough, Mickey was a wanted man. The felony warrant said he was accused of selling football gambling cards from catering trucks, a common, not terribly original scam.

They returned to Brandy's, and there was Mickey. They busted him.

But at the station, Mickey looked like a man

headed for the gallows—like they'd taken him down for a triple homicide or something. When they interrogated the terrified De Petro, he crumbled immediately.

"I can tell you something really good," he said, "a contract murder. But you gotta let me off." And sure enough, he began to give them details about a recent homicide, and his information checked out. This was too bizarre to be true. Why would somebody try to get off the hook on a petty bookmaking rap by rolling over on a murder that might even implicate him?

No judge would have made him serve time on the gambling charge. It was a felony, but one the courts treated like a parking ticket. All he had to do was hire a lawyer and cop a plea. It didn't make sense. But Rothmiller had been a cop long enough now to know just how often people failed to make sense. Sometimes they just reached a point where they couldn't stand the aggravation, and De Petro appeared to be at that point. In his mind, he had expanded the gambling rap into a much bigger problem than it really was.

The two OCID men were visibly excited. An hour ago they were just sitting in a bar doing nothing special, and now they were solving a contract killing. They loved it.

Just by chance, months ago Rothmiller had driven past the murder scene De Petro told them about. Rothmiller hadn't known it was a murder at the time. No one did. There was a car flipped over on the freeway and its driver was dead. The California Highway Patrol (CHP), which handled the case, assumed the death was just the result of a traffic accident. CHP wasn't used to handling homicides. But then an autopsy showed the "traffic" victim had a head full of double-0 buckshot.

Mickey claimed to know all about it. And he did. The victim had worked in a small repair shop next to the Northeast division station. According to Mickey, his widow, who moved to Florida afterward, had hired the hit for $20,000 so she could collect $50,000 in insurance money. Mickey said he worked the job with another lowlife, Max Mayberry.

Mickey claimed he only sat in the backseat. When they pulled alongside the victim, it was Mayberry who'd pulled the trigger. No one heard the shotgun over the noise of the trucks rolling along the freeway. It had almost been the perfect murder.

As time went on, Mickey, promised a break on his two-bit gambling jam, started rolling over on all sorts of other cases. He was a guy who kept his ear to the ground. He turned up gambling operations, hijackings, extortion, a whole array of rackets. And he remembered names, dates, details. He turned out to be a gem of an informant, an investigator's dream.

Meanwhile, the two OCID men stayed in touch with Rothmiller. They still didn't provide many details about their unit, but they were warming up to him. They were more forthcoming than they'd been before the Mickey Rooney bust. They told Rothmiller OCID was a terrific place to work. Detectives called a lot of their own shots and were given more latitude than detectives in other departments.

They often chose their own cases, their own hours and locations. They knew Rothmiller was up for promotion to detective soon. He ought to apply to the unit, they said. Openings came up only every few years, because no one ever quit the unit. But there happened to be an opening now.

Anyone in the department who saw how OCID men worked could see these guys wrote their own ticket in the LAPD. Whoever they were chasing—and Rothmiller could only assume they concentrated their efforts on big-time mobsters—they certainly didn't confine their efforts exclusively to car thieves or sex criminals or burglars working within a certain division. That's the way most detectives had to work—boxed into their little specialties. These OCID guys were able to take an expansive approach, the same way racketeers worked their myriad rackets.

Rothmiller did apply for OCID, and learned that many were called and few were chosen. A spot on OCID was a ripe fruit indeed. Rothmiller was told there were about a hundred applicants competing for the one vacancy.

But singing Rothmiller's praises were the two OCID cops who had witnessed him turn a petty everyday bust into a major success. Rothmiller knew there was an element of luck involved, but success always requires luck. Besides, his proficiency ratings were top-notch. He'd made it from patrolman one to patrolman three in just a few years. He sailed through his interviews. But he remembered one line of questioning that proved prophetic:

"How would you feel about not making an arrest every day?"

Vice detectives, the good ones, made lots of arrests.

"That would be okay," Rothmiller answered, "as long as I knew I was working toward something. I guess if you're working big cases, you can't knock off a case a day."

The answer appeared to satisfy his interviewers.

On May 7, 1978, Rothmiller was simultaneously promoted to detective and transferred into OCID, a highly unusual double dose of advancement. He'd beaten out all the experienced detectives angling for the OCID position. Chief Daryl F. Gates presided over Rothmiller's promotion ceremony. He handed the new badge and certificate to the young detective and congratulated him. Gates had been sworn in as the new chief only seven weeks earlier.

Before Rothmiller's transfer to OCID, he and Nancy had moved into an airy, ranch-style home in coastal Orange County, where they still live. It's a solid stucco house set in a quiet, middle-class tract. The neighborhood attracts hard-working, white-collar couples who fight the San Diego Freeway north to offices in L.A. or south to the Edge City of suburban towers set in and around Irvine.

Around here, you'd have to walk for blocks before finding a speck of litter. Cops—society's point men and women in the struggle with man's inhumanity to man—are drawn to neighborhoods like this. There's nothing like a cozy middle-class refuge after a night in one of the graffiti territories that drive cops to drink, divorce, depression, and world-weary numbness.

Ironically, the cops who live in neighborhoods like Rothmiller's are less likely than their neighbors to trust the well-ordered quiet. Used to mucking around in urban swamps, they always half-expect to turn over something that stinks.

But for Rothmiller, things seemed to be moving in the right direction. He had a new house and a new assignment in an elite unit. Now he would have the opportunity to broaden his investigative skills and focus them on bringing down big-time mobsters. At least that's what he expected.

Inside the
Files

A new detective in the Organized Crime Intelligence Unit was always assigned to work the first several weeks inside the office. In theory, this was supposed to give the newcomer a feel for how the unit operated. Rothmiller sat around for a while trying to figure out what he was supposed to do. Finally a lieutenant approached him with an assignment.

"We need to know how much is in the supply cabinet so we'll know what to order," the lieutenant told him. "Go in there and inventory everything." Not terribly exciting detective work, but Rothmiller began. After a while the lieutenant came back, watched him studiously awhile, and then said, "On those pencils, we need a little better idea. Write how far down they've been used."

"Excuse me?"

"You know, if a pencil's been sharpened, estimate if it's seventy-five percent left, or fifty percent, or what have you. Put all that down on the sheet."

Rothmiller assumed he was being hazed; it was

some kind of initiation rite into OCID. Maybe next they would glue his coffee cup to the desk or something, then all come out laughing. He did what he was told on the pencils and waited for the next zinger. But it never came, because the lieutenant had been serious. The guy wasn't a *real* lieutenant, he was a *pogue* lieutenant.

But the task helped Rothmiller understand the situation. There was really nothing for him to do in the office. He was only working inside because of some time-honored stupidity initiated long ago by some long-retired pogue. No supervisor since had the guts or initiative to change it.

So after inventorying everything in the supply cabinet and counting and measuring all the pencils, he decided to spend his time looking busy. Four lieutenants and a captain worked in this office, and if he looked busy, each of them would think one of the others had assigned him some kind of flunky project and leave him alone.

Not thirty feet from Rothmiller's desk was an entire wall of files. He walked over, pulled open a filing cabinet, and began to read.

He discovered that the files along this wall were composed only of index cards with names on them and codes to indicate where there were other files on each name. He couldn't believe the numbers involved. There were thousands and thousands of names. Could there be this many people in Southern California connected to organized crime?

He started reading names. He learned the key to the codes and the locations of the other files. He had free rein. The files were vaster than he could possibly have imagined. And the names were clearly not all names of organized crime figures.

Most of the names he didn't recognize. Then he started looking for names of famous people. They were all there. Name any celebrity who lived in L.A. or didn't live in L.A. The names were all here:

politicians, movie stars, and sports figures. Along with some criminals. And cross files. Marilyn Monroe crossed, of course, with the Kennedys.

Rothmiller read the detailed file on Bobby Kennedy. Investigators accounted for ten spent .22-caliber slugs in the kitchen of the Ambassador Hotel where RFK was shot dead. Sirhan Sirhan's revolver held eight bullets. Nowhere did the file draw any conclusions about the discrepancy.

OCID detectives had collected an enormous pack of raw data on Frank Sinatra, the Rat Pack, and the Rat Pack family tree (Nancy, Frank, Jr., all of them). When Los Angeles Lakers owner Jerry Busse had a new girlfriend, OCID wanted to know.

Looking through the OCID files turned out to be detective work after all. They were a raw repository of the human comedy, a weird compilation of indicators and counterindicators that led places and no place at all. Poring through them was like clicking through thousands of cable channels: image after image, facts, rumors, suppositions. Most of it was unsubstantiated gossip. And some of the stuff that was substantiated was just plain silly: Don Rickles played Caesars Palace on such and such a date.

Dead people had entries in their file made years after their demise because of the elaborate cross-filing system. A dead Joe X had been a partner of a living Joe Y, who had just been surveillanced, so both of them received new entries. Contrary to supermarket rags, Elvis is no doubt dead. But not his OCID file.

There were files upon files describing Rock Hudson's gay trysts. Who cared? Even if someone in the LAPD were out to squeeze allegiance out of Hudson, enough was enough. How many nuclear missiles did it take to destroy the world? Besides which, what did all this stuff have to do with organized crime?

OCID paid tremendous attention to the entertainment industry. Dino De Laurentiis, for instance, had an enormous number of entries in his file. Although this was puzzling at first, the reason would later become clear. Hollywood notables were essentially a trivial aristocracy around much of the world. But in L.A. they were leaders of a powerful homegrown industry. The OCID files showed a clear bias toward getting information on the powerful. With this knowledge came more power for the LAPD.

They were little more than voyeurs. OCID had the resources and so it was nice to know who was bedding whom before *People* magazine told everyone else. It simply made the owner of this information feel that much more important.

But power remained the watchword in these files. Those who had power over money or politics or labor unions or mass media were watched carefully. No suspicions of criminal activity were necessary.

A typically enormous file was the one on former Governor Edmund G. "Pat" Brown. Business deals, acquaintances, the standard kind of stuff investigators would gather if they wanted every scrap of information on someone.

The file on his son, Jerry Brown, was clearer in purpose: prove he's gay. There was, for example, an unsubstantiated report that the bedroom walls in his apartment in L.A.'s Fairfax district were painted black in the then-preferred manner of sadomasochistic freaks. The files showed eavesdropping on his car phone conversations, intensive surveillance at the apartment. Results? Absolutely nothing confirmed.

In the six weeks that followed, Rothmiller performed occasional research chores in the OCID office, such as checking to see who paid the utilities on a particular address. But he had lots of time on his hands. As detectives and pogues walked in and out and around the office, Rothmiller dug deeper into the enormous accumulation of files and asked himself: What kind of police unit is this anyway?

The index card file at OCID contained names and indicators to reports found in several rows of floor-to-ceiling shelves. These held intelligence files dating back to the 1930s, though the reports held little substance, only basic surveillance and intelligence data that no doubt would be released if subpoenaed.

But a misplaced asterisk somewhere in the description of a particular file meant that a matching report also existed, similarly numbered. In a separate, locked room just a few feet from the main filing shelves were reports containing the actual confidential information. Known as the "CF" files, these reports chronicled the years of intelligence gathering, half-baked theories, suppositions, shaggy dog stories, and countless dirty tricks relating to anyone of substance, importance, or newsworthiness in L.A. and many points beyond.

Some targeted individuals had up to forty index cards on file with each card representing twenty to twenty-five intelligence reports. The system meant an especially sensitive report could disappear without a trace simply by removing a 3-by-5 card from the master index, making it no longer an "official file" for subpoena purposes. Without the card, it would be impossible for any searcher to wade through hundreds of thousands of reports to find the right one. And in any case, the true file was the CF file—a file that didn't exist to anyone outside OCID.

To make the files even more impenetrable to court orders and the like, there was a third, even *more* confidential file put together just in case an outsider somehow gained access to the CF file. This supremely sensitive stuff—much of it consisting of the files detailing investigations of people not suspected of crimes—would be spirited off OCID premises years later, after Rothmiller was a division veteran.

This supersecret set of files was put together as an emergency measure because at the time, the ACLU was hot on the trail of Public Disorder Intelligence Division files to find evidence of political espionage. The third set of OCID files was organized alphabetically into twenty-six sets—one for each letter of the alphabet. Each lettered file was transported to a public storage unit rented in the name of a detective and paid for in cash. There was also a plan in place to change storage units every year. This stuff would be impossible to trace unless one of these key detectives with the key to the kingdom rolled over on any of the locations.

Captain Stuart Finck, then the OCID commander, approached Rothmiller while the detectives were feverishly putting together the third file. He asked how everything was proceeding.

"Well, there's a lot of stuff to go through," Rothmiller responded.

"The one thing I dread is the day an ACLU attorney gets into the files," Finck said. "That would be the day the entire lid is blown off the police department."

The captain gestured toward the departing files and explained that from now on, "These don't exist. These are not files."

If just having this stuff in their possession was so frightening, why didn't these people just destroy the files? The answer would have to be that they wanted them in case they ever needed them for something in the future. These files so painstakingly put together over the years were hot potatoes, but they were also seen as an asset worth the risk. Like storing seven years' worth of grain in the cellar. You never knew.

Once the supersecret third file was created, the detectives went back to the master file index where asterisks were added to denote sensitive files and they crossed out the indicators with a black marking pen. Now if someone subpoenaed any of those ghost files, the official response could be that the file was irrelevant and therefore destroyed or that it was no longer an official LAPD file.

The money used to pay for the storage units was taken from a cash fund called the Secret Service Fund that was earmarked for incidental expenses and payoffs to informants.

But that wasn't the end to the file maze. Because there was even a fourth set of intelligence files— kept by the chief. It consisted of notes and paper briefings that were not written on standard LAPD intelligence file forms. Hence, they were called "white papers." The white papers were not official LAPD documents, so how could anyone subpoena them? They would not be presented to a court because they were just scraps of paper, not files.

Many of the white papers were assembled by the chief's political team, the two-man political espionage unit within OCID. If they thought they had something hot enough, the two operatives presented it directly to Gates, although the captain had been known to protest the arrangement.

Not far from the officially nonexistent CF files was a fair-sized room where OCID stored its electronic gear. Two electronics specialists known around the division as Boris and Igor did nothing but monitor and care for this equipment. Most of it could not be used legally, but there it was. Spike mikes, for instance, designed to be punched into a wall to bug a room. It was absolutely illegal for any of California's police agencies to employ a bug as evidence unless the bug was a "wire" worn by a person. (Bugs record conversations in physical locations; taps record telephone conversations.)

But as Gates, an ex-OCID captain, has conceded, the division used bugs anyway "for our own edification." Given the time-honored LAPD practice of fictionalizing reports, it was therefore relatively easy to use information from these bugs, contending later that the information came from another source.

As for police telephone taps, they were illegal in California, although a 1989 ruling would later allow court-ordered taps under unusual circumstances.

Perhaps Gates wasn't aware of it, but OCID detectives were very much aware that bugging and tapping were felonies. Therefore, these practices were not readily admitted to—not even in a former detective's own book. Putting a tail on Tony Curtis or Senator Alan Cranston might bring heat if it were known, but it would not necessarily trigger criminal charges. If a detective ever admitted that he did in fact bug rooms and tap lines illegally during the course of his investigations, he would be confessing to a felony that could saddle him with both criminal and civil charges. Still, suffice it to say that electronic surveillance was very much a part of OCID then—as it is now.

Administrative Vice and Administrative Narcotics, the central divisions that handled big operations in these respective fields of crime, also had their own bugging and tapping equipment. But if they wanted to use it, they practically needed the king's signet. In OCID, detectives had freer rein, pretty much doing whatever they felt needed to be done.

Bugging became almost a way of life in OCID. Everyone always assumed anything said inside the office could be picked up by somebody else's device. The detectives bugged their own captain and lieutenants. There was a fraternity-prank atmosphere to some of this, but it was also deadly serious. The credo was: Get something on anyone who can affect your job situation. For instance, someone left some surveillance photos on the desk of a lieutenant. He was having an extramarital affair, and the photos were of his favorite motel.

Detectives also routinely picked the desk locks of the two-man political team to find out what they were working on, what the latest quiet teams were up to. Because the political team members affected a hush-hush attitude, this was seen as a direct challenge to their colleagues. Their response was to spy on the team that spied on the politicians.

After Rothmiller had spent a few weeks stalking the secrets of the files, a supervisor asked him about his polygraph test.

"Polygraph test?" Rothmiller said. "What polygraph test?"

This sparked an OCID anxiety attack. No one was supposed to get into the unit, much less its files, without first passing a lie detector test. He was rushed into one that afternoon.

Many detectives who would otherwise apply for OCID gave it a pass because of the polygraph hurdle, designed to screen out drunks, gays, dopers, ex-dopers, psychos, mob moles, media sources, sex kinks, and other miscreants who'd made it into the LAPD. There was a one-way mirror in the polygraph room, and the person being tested had no idea who might be watching on the other side.

The polygraph man asked the usual questions: "Have you ever stolen anything?"

"Yeah, when I was a kid."

And so on. Then Rothmiller was asked: "Did you ever lie to a department supervisor?"

He answered affirmatively. He had lied, and

everyone else had too. When a supervisor asked an officer about the behavior of another cop, if the cop was in the wrong, the officer lied. He was expected to lie. The supervisor expected him to lie. "No, I didn't see a thing." Or "That's right, he didn't strike the suspect until after the suspect tried to hit him first."

Rothmiller passed the polygraph test.

After he'd done his weeks in the office, Rothmiller was finally allowed to work the next step in OCID: airport detail. LAPD higher-ups wanted to know who was coming in and out of L.A., and this little intelligence activity was part of OCID's routine. Of particular interest were the identities of any notables coming from or leaving for Las Vegas.

Chief Gates once told Lew Wasserman, longtime chairman of the MCA entertainment conglomerate: "We knew every time you boarded a plane for Las Vegas." Gates claimed this surveillance was for the protection of people in the entertainment industry. The LAPD was watching over them to make sure they were not victimized by the Mafia, he explained. George Orwell's Big Brother also watched over all his citizens for their own good.

The fact is, when cops like Gates bragged to others they had gathered personal details about their lives, even if this were communicated in a friendly way, the message and the intent were anything but friendly.

Airport detail was not exactly a plum assignment in OCID. It was the kind of low-level surveillance activity reserved mostly for newcomers and detectives who didn't produce much. Still, Rothmiller was delighted to get out of the office and do something more related to the work of a detective.

In 1978, when Rothmiller started work in OCID, Western Airlines, which later would become one of the industry's deregulation victims, flew most of the flights between Los Angeles International Airport and McCarran International Airport in Las Vegas. The six to eight OCID detectives detailed to LAX were a familiar sight to Western employees and they were given free run of the facilities.

Western employees even trained them to use the airline's computer system so they could personally check names, flights, and other data. On many occasions, passengers, seeing the detectives punching away at a computer terminal, would take them for airline employees and request a change in seat assignment or something.

The cops would generally nod, smile, keep punching away, and then say it was all taken care of, although of course they hadn't done anything of the kind. This was a running joke on the airport detail, one that may not have caused the airline's eventual demise but certainly didn't do much to prevent it either.

When the detectives were interested in a name they saw on a flight list, they might set up a surveillance or arrange to take some surreptitious photographs. Every time they saw such a name they made out a report. It might just be a terse statement saying Barbra Streisand flew out of LAX on such and such a flight—or it could go much further. It might show that before her departure, the detectives followed Streisand into the VIP lounge, where she was met by a man believed to be her agent, and that the two were then overheard talking about a possible movie project with Robert Redford. Just the sort of information Los Angeles taxpayers wanted their police officers pursuing in order to prevent a crime wave.

While working the airport detail, Rothmiller got a firsthand look at how casually OCID detectives roamed beyond legal barriers. Not long after he began the assignment, Rothmiller and an OCID supervisor followed the now-deceased Morris Shenker into the Horizon Club, a Western Airlines executive lounge. Shenker was then principal owner of the Dunes Hotel and Casino in Las Vegas.

While sitting with a group of associates, Shenker picked up a telephone to place a call. Rothmiller's supervisor got up and motioned to Rothmiller to follow. They proceeded to another area where there was a telephone console. The supervisor removed the mouthpiece and picked up the line to listen in, which was absolutely illegal.

In the banal report on this incident, the supervisor would later write that Shenker had called his wife in Las Vegas and asked after his grandchildren. This was just the first of many times Rothmiller would witness this eavesdropping tactic at the airport.

OCID men would pop the locks of cars parked at the airport and rummage through their interiors. If they knew a group of more than routine interest to OCID was headed toward a particular car, they would sometimes let the air out of a tire. This would always cause everyone in the group to stand around and stare at the tire awhile. Human nature. Never failed. That way the OCID men got better photographs.

All of this might have been an eye-opener to a newcomer, but after six years on the LAPD it was no shock—just another box of tricks used by the department against the citizens it was supposed to serve and protect. Once a cop learned somehow to accept working alongside officers who were deranged bullies, he was not likely to draw the line at a flattened tire on airport detail.

But Rothmiller did begin to ask other questions. Most patrol officers, after all, were not psychos, and during his previous LAPD duties Rothmiller could tell himself that the city was better off with this police force than with no police force at all. But waiting at the airport to see when Liberace's plane came in, it was easy to begin wondering just how important this Organized Crime Intelligence Division was to the City of Los Angeles. Could OCID justify its existence? And if it couldn't, what was he doing working here?

After four months of seasoning him at the airport, the OCID chieftains decided it was safe to let Rothmiller go out on the streets and work some cases. But as a new man, of course, he should partner with a veteran who knew his way around. He was teamed up with a hard-charging investigator, one of their best men.

(In OCID, "detective" and "man" were practically interchangeable terms. During his five years aboard the OCID team, Rothmiller saw only one woman detective allowed to work in the unit. The supervisors never let her out of the office. Eventually she transferred out of the unit—becoming an exception to the rule that no one ever voluntarily left OCID.)

Rothmiller, who hadn't done any real detective work in almost half a year, was delighted. He'd been hoping and planning for this eventuality, and now it had finally arrived. He could go out and build cases against L.A.'s biggest mobsters.

Teamed up with this veteran detective, he knew better than to appear overeager. He just wanted to do well. He knew he was good at this. He was a good detective and now he'd be able to prove it.

Under the tutelage of his new partner, Rothmiller first attacked a case pertaining to Vans shoes. Vans athletic shoes were all the rage then, and the detective's teenage son craved a pair. This called for much study.

After a couple of hours spent researching the question, Rothmiller's superdetective partner drove out to find some Vans shoes flunkies at the factory and headquarters in Anaheim. But he didn't get what he was after. So he decided to approach this one head-on. Using his OCID identification, the master sleuth bluffed his way in to see the president of the company.

"My son really likes your company's shoes," the detective began. It didn't take very long for the president, wise to the ways of the world, to comprehend what these two schnorrers were after. He had to decide whether it was worth it to ask them to leave, or, what the hell, give them their goddamn shoes. He gave them the shoes. They were worth about twenty dollars. They cost the citizens of Los Angeles a day's pay for two detectives.

This brand of blatant panhandling existed as a sort of throwback to the thirties and forties, when the department was famous for its thieving finaglers. Rothmiller's new partner did everything in his power to keep the old tradition alive.

The veteran's next project was even more ambitious. He was having all the landscaping redone outside his suburban Lake Forest residence. The job would include an elaborate new hot tub and deck. He needed to get a long list of materials free—or at worst, wholesale.

With Rothmiller in the car, he spent almost an entire day just lining up the best deal on some PCV pipe for his irrigation system, always waving his OCID connections around as though it were the Medal of Honor.

PCV piping is extremely cheap, and several times Rothmiller wanted to just volunteer to pay for it himself to get this over with. But he held his tongue. This guy was his supervisor, after all. It seemed every time things in OCID were about to start looking up, Rothmiller had to turn his head and ignore something new.

Rothmiller learned it was much easier for OCID detectives to embezzle time and flake off than anywhere else he'd worked in the department.

Their cases were freewheeling, and they didn't have to make arrests. They were allowed to roam all over Southern California, too. No need to hang around inside L.A. if there was a better deal on fence lumber somewhere else.

His partner would just call in and say he was going to be out of radio range all day. Then later on, he would read through the newspapers and write "intelligence" reports based on some articles. On the form, he would just label the source of his information as an unverified statement from an anonymous informant. That would cover it.

Other times he would come into the office, ask other detectives what they were working on, then sign his name on their reports as an assisting investigator. He was crafty enough always to make a joke of it. The other detectives knew it wasn't quite a joke, but they went along.

"This guy's into everything," the pogues would say, reading all the reports. For pogues were always more trusting of paper than reality. And that's how they came to believe he was a great detective, exactly the sort of man they wanted for steering Rothmiller around as he broke into the serious business of being an intelligence detective.

At one point Rothmiller's partner spent an entire salaried month at home supervising the landscaping job. Employing a less severe version of the scam Rothmiller's old vice sergeant had used against his undocumented housekeeper, this guy hired two undocumented laborers to dig the hole for his hot tub, then flashed his badge when they were finished. Take off, he told them, which they did without pay.

Eventually Rothmiller could make an educated estimate of just how much work was being done in the unit. He figured at least half the detectives settled for the easy life and were completely worthless. They would bluff their way through nonexistent cases of their own and then, when they had to, assist other detectives on a surveillance.

Most of the other detectives were capable of spurts of determination from time to time. A very small number of the investigators were out there every day pursuing actual criminal suspects. This so-called elite LAPD division had to be the laziest, least productive unit in the whole department.

Rothmiller was determined to join the company of the productive sliver. But first he'd have to get out from under the pogues and the hot-tub detective.

· 7 ·

Take Your Tan and Shove It

Rothmiller noticed a few rare detectives in OCID who had little patience for the sopho-moric skulking around after celebrities and other potentates that was so much a part of the unit's day-to-day mission. One of them was a trim, brainy veteran by the name of Frank Skrah. Skrah knew how to make the pogues uncomfortable. He spoke up at meetings and was not afraid to challenge a silly order.

Several of the other detectives had warned Rothmiller about Skrah. They said he was a pain in the ass, a martinet, difficult to get along with. Then, after Rothmiller had worked in the unit several months, the powers that be teamed him up with Skrah. Although Rothmiller was delighted to get away finally from the shop-till-he-dropped hot-tub detective, he feared he might be going from the frying pan to the fire on this one.

After they became partners, Rothmiller found Skrah, who was about ten years older, to be a friendly, honest man with a good sense of humor.

He also happened to be a highly skilled detective. It explained why so many of his colleagues didn't like him. He wanted to solve crimes, which interfered with their laid-back semiretirement.

Like too many civil servants, a good many LAPD cops figured they would get paid whether they worked hard or not. But in OCID, there were so many ways to flake off, anyone who stood in the way of this very reachable Nirvana was treated like the antichrist.

Also, Rothmiller understood now why the pogues put up with Skrah's renegade behavior. Even they recognized that every once in a while it might pay to have someone around who could actually produce.

Teamed with Skrah, Rothmiller began investigating real criminals again. He and his new partner managed to do this the same way Rothmiller had dodged the office pogue who once ordered him to sort pencils—they looked busy. But this time Rothmiller really was busy. He discovered that when he worked legitimate cases, more often than not he could dodge the silly missions passed down by the pogues. Rothmiller, who had resuscitated his Mike Lange role, kept his ear to the ground and began to turn in intelligence reports that actually dealt with organized crime figures.

The LAPD had been bragging for years that due to its unmatchable police work, the mob had barely a toehold in Southern California. And it was true that the old-line syndicate didn't wield as much power in L.A. as it did in cities back East. But this didn't tell the whole story. Southern California had traditional mobsters committing their traditional crimes, but they altered their tactics in L.A. because of the different circumstances.

Among these traditional racketeers were transferees—thugs like Jimmy "the Weasel" Fratianno—who had been dispatched to Southern

California as mob-style branch officers for their bosses in Chicago. Over the years the mob had been expanding its activities to new crimes, particularly during the seventies. Southern California became more of a Chicago syndicate preserve because mobsters from Chicago liked to winter in Palm Springs, while mobsters from New York preferred Florida.

While they were in their winter quarters, they figured they might as well make some money. Nearby L.A. was a natural target for their activities. Some of the snowbirds who did well in California even stopped going back to Chicago. They became Californians. That was the California story. It was a place that drew all kinds of people from all over.

Chicago mob boss Tony Acardo had a winter home in Palm Springs. His Chicago area phone records, which Rothmiller checked out, showed he would periodically call a Palm Springs home next to his winter residence. It belonged to a Los Angeles manufacturer. Rothmiller looked him over. He was completely clean. Rothmiller thought the man might be in some sort of jeopardy, so he called on him.

As it turned out, the neighbor had no idea Acardo was a racketeer. They were just golfing buddies—two men from different worlds who took a liking to each other. And sometimes when Acardo was in the Chicago area the two of them would chew the fat over the telephone wire.

But the man said he began to suspect Acardo wielded unusual power after an incident at a country club. The manufacturer had left a very valuable German camera in his car, which the valet had parked for him. When the owner returned, the camera had disappeared. He couldn't get anyone at the country club to take responsibility. They just shined him on. Not our problem, they said. He had pretty much given up already when Acardo stopped by.

"I told him what had happened," the man recalled for Rothmiller, "and he said, 'Let me see if I can help.' Tony drove over there himself. An hour later I received a call from the head maitre d' at the club. He said they had found my camera. The valet did it and he was fired. They were suddenly very apologetic. Couldn't do enough for me. The maitre d' brought it right over. 'Please have a free dinner on us,' he said."

After Rothmiller explained just who Acardo was, the man was ready to panic. "My God," he said, "do you think we're in danger here? Should I sell the house?" Rothmiller smiled. "I'm sure you're in no danger at all," he said.

Operating in L.A., mob guys learned to change tactics. In many cases they became legitimate businessmen who pulled capers on the side. They didn't have big crews of mob soldiers, so they weren't quick to use strongarm tactics. Instead, they leaned toward white-collar scams that relied more on stealth and finesse.

For example, back East, or in the Midwest, rackets guys would muscle their way into a legitimate business, then "bust it out"—order tons of merchandise for the business, then sell the stuff cheap and duck out, leaving their legitimate "partners" with the bills. The primary ingredient in these bustouts was the victims' fear of retaliation. In California, mobsters would use the bustout scam but with a con-artist twist.

They wouldn't muscle their way into the business. Instead they might "buy" it. Posing as legitimate investors, they would make a $500,000 down payment on a stereo store that held $10 million in merchandise, promising the balance in thirty days. But they would have to take over immediately.

Then they would order more merchandise worth more millions, using the owner's lines of credit with the wholesalers. With new wares pouring into the store, they would sell everything fast, at half-price, even less. What's the difference? They paid only $500,000 for the entire stock. Then they would disappear, leaving the bills for the former owner.

Or they might set up an import-export office somewhere, have business cards printed up, and begin ordering computer chips from a manufacturer. They would make several small orders, always paying up front. After establishing a relationship with the manufacturer, they would then order a huge quantity of chips, pledging payment ten days after delivery. Ten days after delivery there would be nothing but an empty office where the export-import business used to be.

Usually by the time the cops found out, the owners were sitting numb in the ruins, holding the proverbial bag. But there were times cops had information beforehand and refused to move. If the businessman was from the wrong ethnic group, then he was probably a crook too, the cops figured. Let him take the fall.

This was akin to the tactics and philosophy of another secretive LAPD unit called the Special Investigations Section. This nineteen-man force was assigned to watch armed robbers and burglars who were repeat offenders. But although section operatives would watch their targets illegally assembling weapons and preparing to pounce on somebody, they rarely made any arrests until the jobs were being pulled and citizens were in critical danger.

Then the cops would blast their way in, often killing their prey. The LAPD called it a fine example of proactive policing. Critics called it an assassination squad.

Meanwhile, when it came to scams, the old-line mobsters didn't have a monopoly over them. L.A., with its surge of immigrants from distant lands, was fast becoming the new ethnic melting pot of America. And some among these immigrants—Chinese, Vietnamese, Arabs, Mexicans, Central Americans, Israelis, Cubans—were racketeers from home. They pulled their old capers and learned new ones, too. Clearly there was a need for racket busters in L.A. The question was whether OCID was up to the job.

One day Rothmiller, reading over some reports filed by the airport detail, noticed that a man by the name of Sam Sarcinelli had drawn some attention at the terminal. He was booked for a flight to Florida, and when he opened his briefcase to remove the ticket, he revealed a wad of cash inside estimated at $20,000.

Rothmiller did some checking on this Sarcinelli and discovered there was a Sam Sarcinelli in the Chicago mob who was a lieutenant of Mafia chieftain Tony Acardo. Further checks showed that this same Sarcinelli had lately taken up residence in Laguna Beach, just down the coast a few miles from Rothmiller's home. It was common for OCID detectives to find someone they could keep an eye on who lived near their homes. Then they could just call in in the morning and they were on the job. No miserable commute to the division office downtown. "I'm watching my guy. I think he may be up to something this morning."

Of course Laguna Beach was outside the city, but that wouldn't matter. OCID detectives didn't need much of an L.A. connection to pursue a case. They roamed throughout Southern California and beyond, styling themselves as a kind of regional intelligence agency.

As Rothmiller began checking out Sarcinelli, he

discovered a guy who was always up to something. The Chicago transplant was a wheeler-dealer who couldn't seem to get into enough situations. He had his fingers in real estate transactions, construction, gambling, and he was just getting into narcotics when Rothmiller and Skrah began watching him. Sarcinelli, a glib string bean of a man with a quick, easy manner, could easily have played the part of a potato broker or an appliance salesman.

Eventually he would lease a Learjet, hire a crew, and start making runs to various places around the country, usually stopping in Florida first. It didn't take a lot of figuring to suspect he was selling drugs.

He also would meet with a chieftain of the Outlaws biker gang who lived in the San Fernando Valley—"Crazy Frank" Salcido. Salcido went along on several of the jet trips. This puzzled the two investigators. What did these two see in each other? As it turned out, the detectives were among the first cops to stumble upon the new phenomenon of old-line racketeers and biker gangs hooking up to commit crimes. The racketeers had connections to financing and drugs. The bikers knew where to sell the drugs and they could provide sorely needed muscle.

Muscle was scarce partly because success had been a double-edged sword for the American Mafia. As mobsters made money, they joined the middle-class migration to the suburbs. Their children were more interested in sports, computer games, and rock concerts than in fighting and stealing, the building blocks of gangster life. Desperate for talent, old-line racketers had to look elsewhere for thugs. Sometimes they even sent back to Italy for recruits.

Eventually, Sarcinelli would move out of Laguna Beach and establish an office in Sherman Oaks, about sixty miles north in the San Fernando Valley.

Rothmiller stayed with him. As Sarcinelli's enterprises mushroomed, investigating him took more and more of the detective's time.

Rothmiller would start looking into one matter, which would lead to other schemes, other criminals, who would further lead him to still new connections. These connections were more a web than a long string. A detective could get lost in them as one scam led to others in a tortured convolution of relationships and betrayals.

Rothmiller and his partner "trashed" Sarcinelli for years, that is, bribed the trash men with twenty dollars a week so they would set aside his refuse in carefully marked bags. Sarcinelli never caught on to this, and the two detectives often knew, by reading through the scraps, what the mobster was going to do before he did it.

The detectives would bring the trash to the nearest police station in Van Nuys to sift through it. This created lots of suspicion and questions from station pogues. Rothmiller and Ken Hamilton, his partner in the latter part of his OCID career, refused to tell them anything. Eventually the Van Nuys captain called the OCID captain because he feared the two OCID men were trashing his division. It was a good lesson on the state of intradepartmental paranoia within the LAPD.

Rothmiller also set up surveillances outside Sarcinelli's office. He observed him freebasing cocaine dozens of times. Watching through a night vision scope, he would see a sudden eerie flash inside and know that his target was getting firehigh.

Freebasing is by itself a felony, but of course the supervisors of the much-vaunted Organized Crime Intelligence Division would never stand for busting Sarcinelli. It would spell an end to their beloved intelligence reports. They made it abundantly clear to Rothmiller that they would crucify him if he cut off this fount of information with anything as crude as an arrest.

So Rothmiller and his partner kept watching and waiting. Meanwhile, they gummed up the works in Sarcinelli's schemes. Trashing treated them to pungent piles of notes, dates, contacts, meeting times, phone numbers, and the like, which they immediately funneled back to other agencies such as the U.S. Drug Enforcement Agency in Chicago, which would then discreetly leak the information out on the street. Within hours news of the leak would make its way back to California. The idea was to make sure no one trusted anyone else.

Sarcinelli, who was probably paranoid anyway from his liberal cocaine use, would get frantic after these episodes. He was convinced someone had bugged his office. The two detectives would observe him from across the street as he disassembled his furniture in search of a microphone that didn't exist. Increasingly desperate, he suspected that some enemy had somehow planted a bug inside his dog. He took it to the veterinarian for a full-body X ray. A detective's life could be sweet.

Then came the day when out of the Sarcinelli trash Rothmiller and Hamilton fished the text for a classified ad. Their man was going to advertise for an assistant! Bull's-eye. A perfect opportunity to get somebody inside. What Sarcinelli wanted was a bright, attractive woman to take care of his office chores and answer the phone with a little class.

The two detectives knew they needed a good undercover officer to fill the bill. But they also knew the OCID pogues would never spring for it. This was just a criminal case with no political overtones. Even if they would have considered the tactic seriously, by the time everything went through the proper LAPD channels, the cows would come home. No, only the feds had the resources for this.

The two detectives had been trading their Sarcinelli information to other agencies for some time. Because this particular mobster's biggest emphasis was on drugs, probably the DEA would be the likeliest candidate to work with on this one. But although they had DEA contacts, all right, DEA wasn't their first choice. There was one FBI agent, Bill Ryan, of the San Fernando Valley office, who inspired more of Rothmiller's trust.

Like so many city detectives, Rothmiller placed little faith in the FBI. He saw its agents mostly as a collection of lawyers and accountants by training who tried their best to create a network of informants. But they didn't have the street wisdom to sift nuggets of truth from the lies criminals were so happy to pass on to unsuspecting cops. Still, after the decades of brilliant publicity engineered by their decidedly odd founder, J. Edgar Hoover, they were always quick to pop in front of a camera somewhere and take credit for a city cop's work.

But Ryan was the exception to the rule, and in less than a day he got approval; the FBI would try to plant a mole in Sarcinelli's office. Aware when and where the ad would appear, that first morning they had three female FBI agents ready to seek the job. Sarcinelli hired the first one he interviewed— an attractive agent of Japanese descent. She would remain in the Sherman Oaks office for six months, watching every move from the inside, sabotaging Sarcinelli's schemes, filing reports, reaping invaluable information on just how the mob worked—and dodging Sarcinelli's romantic overtures.

Meanwhile, Rothmiller and Hamilton, without telling the FBI, kept trashing the office anyway, just in case the FBI wasn't giving them straight accounts on Sarcinelli. That was common in the cop business. A cop might trust individuals in other police agencies, but never that police agency. The individual the cop trusted might be under orders to shine the cop on, which meant the cop didn't trust even the people he trusted.

Sarcinelli wasn't the only item on Rothmiller's menu. Along with cops from other agencies, he spent time investigating a mob push to legalize gambling at Lake Havasu City, Arizona. What did this have to do with Los Angeles? Not a great deal, at least directly. But his bosses liked to receive good intelligence, and he liked to investigate big criminal cases. And it was certainly of more value to Los Angeles citizens than tailing celebrities down Santa Monica Boulevard.

On this Arizona scheme, the mobs in Chicago and New York were cooperating—as were Teamster officials who thought a new gambling Mecca could create lucrative investment opportunities for their union coffers. The mobs had already agreed on how to divvy up the action if they could just push this through.

The original goal had been to legalize gambling statewide, turning Arizona into another Nevada. But when this proved impossible, the mob set its sights on Lake Havasu City on the California line. It was even closer to the population centers of Southern California than Las Vegas, and would, the mob dreamed, open up an entire new territory for profits.

There was much at stake, and the campaign grew ugly in Arizona. Opponents were getting muscled. Rothmiller was drawing information from his informants and trading it with cops elsewhere for what they had. That was an integral part of cop intelligence work—trading with other agencies.

But just about everybody's informants were pulling some kind of scam, and problems arose whenever cop number one from another agency zeroed in on the capers of an informant belonging to cop number two. Cop number two would have to weigh the factors. What was his guy into? How good had his information been lately? And just how nasty was this caper that cop number one was chasing him for?

Sometimes cops dummied up to protect their informant, sometimes they decided it was time to throw him to the wolves. Everybody understood the game.

Sometimes Rothmiller would file an intelligence report and get called in quickly by the captain, who, in a belligerent tone, would say, "The chief wants to know why you're interested in this guy." This would tip Rothmiller off to a number of possibilities. Perhaps the chief was keeping a close eye on these intelligence reports. Or, the captain could have been lying and the question might have originated elsewhere, perhaps even from the captain himself. But it was unlikely the captain would have sufficient imagination to try this. The message probably was coming from the chief. And the message was to lay off this particular guy.

Once Rothmiller filed an unverified report that a man named Sam Perricone, Sr., working with a partner, was buying up a lot of oceanfront Orange County real estate. It might not mean anything at all, but the policy was to file such tidbits just in case, particularly since Rothmiller remembered there already was a massive file on Perricone. The Perricone intelligence file was almost as big as Sinatra's—a ton of reports going back for decades.

The day after Rothmiller filed his report, he radioed in to let the office know he was in service. He was told to telephone his captain immediately.

"Can you verify this information?" the captain said, not friendly. Of course he knew the answer, because Rothmiller had checked the "reliability unknown" box on the report. When Rothmiller told the captain what the captain already knew, the captain chewed him out. "Before you do an investigation on this man, you talk to me first, understand?" The message was clear: Lay off Perricone. Rothmiller said he understood.

Later, Rothmiller mentioned the episode to another OCID detective, who laughed out loud. "Don't you know who Perricone is?"

"Some rich guy who lives in Orange County and has a humongous file," Rothmiller answered.

"His son is married to Gates's daughter," the detective told him, still chuckling. "You don't ever do anything on Perricone. If you do, it goes right to the chief, and the chief gets directly on your ass."

Whoops. Rothmiller returned to the file and examined it more closely. It had stopped growing all of a sudden, as though a big sharp sword had severed all inquiries—no doubt just about the time Gates's daughter Kathy was betrothed.

Later on, Rothmiller discovered that when Kathy Gates became engaged to Perricone's son, Sam Perricone, Jr., two OCID investigators had been ordered to do a detailed background check on the younger Perricone. The old man had put agents on the tail of his own future son-in-law, as though the hapless kid were hooking up with Macbeth's daughter. Trouble and toil.

What would Gates have told his offspring if he didn't like the way the report read? Or was he just assembling information for the same reason he gathered such materials on city council members? Just in case, because you never knew.

The operatives could have asked why Los Angeles taxpayers should be footing the bills for this very personal sleuthing. But the men of OCID had long since learned never to ask such questions.

The chief, OCID men knew, spared no OCID shoe leather to prevent his own embarrassment. Intelligence files listed places as well as names. And the chief's office always wanted updated entries of any restaurant locations frequented by mobsters. A master list was kept in Gates's car so he could avoid them. He didn't want to be caught cutting a steak with some godfather type dining at the next table. It wouldn't look good.

Other names were flagged in OCID files for legitimate reasons. If a detective turned in a report on them he would be told to see the captain, who would then tell the cop to back off. In these legitimate cases, there usually was some other agency, the FBI, perhaps, surveilling the individual, and OCID didn't want to step on someone else's case.

But if a flag was permanently in place, the men knew there was some special personal circumstance at work. They also knew, as they were repeatedly told, that insubordination could get them fired or transferred. Or put on airport detail. Or perhaps worst of all, transferred back inside the office gulag as a permanent file boy.

There was the time a black pimp by the name of Willy Cunningham complained to Skrah that a certain deputy chief was shaking down one of his hookers for free sex. Cunningham was no ordinary pimp. He was a huge, mean, 290-pound, fearless leg breaker, a vicious, street-smart dope dealer and all-around badass who was among the better OCID informants. His stories carried weight.

This was one of those hot potatoes that wasn't so easy to dump off elsewhere. To ignore such a report was to invite big trouble; Rothmiller and Skrah might be accused of assisting the illegal acts of another officer. But to turn in this info could bring down terrible wrath as well. Much depended on how tall this particular deputy chief stood in the royal court.

A charge like this was exactly the sort of material that would be used to destroy the career of an ordinary officer. Although the department was afloat in a sea of street brutality and false reports, at the same time, the Internal Affairs Division, with the help of pogue supervisors from throughout the department, was eager to toss cops into quicksand for just a hint of impropriety.

As it turned out, the assistant chief they took the information to didn't want to hear this particular hint of impropriety. He got up and paced around for a long time, muttering, and finally said, "We'll take care of it from here." But who would do the investigating? It wasn't made clear, of course. The information died right there in the pogue's office. This deputy chief stood tall.

Working within OCID, Rothmiller was fast expanding his contacts in other police agencies. He was taking down more and more suspects by turning them over to other agencies whenever possible. He also resorted to calling a 1-800 phone number that received criminal tips and turned them over to proper authorities. In these cases the proper authorities were often somewhere within the LAPD.

Veteran OCID men knew that if they ever found anyone involved in a homicide, the intelligence pogues would allow an arrest. They drew the line at sitting on their hands when somebody was actually killed or about to be killed. But arrests for mere stealing, doping, smuggling, scamming, and related crimes simply would not do.

Once Rothmiller's captain received a letter from the DEA praising the detective for turning over information on a suspected felon that led to his federal arrest. Of course the captain was not pleased, but he let it go that time.

Normal police procedure was to move right in on a felony. If a cop wanted to milk that particular crook for information, one of the best ways to get it was to make an arrest and get a conviction. Once the offender was on probation or parole, he was easy to jerk around and turn into an informant. But

OCID cops were forced to operate differently, as though information, not arrests and convictions, were the true object of police investigations. It called for a different mindset. The reasons for this were never spelled out. But whenever someone suggested making an arrest, the supervisors acted as if he were recommending they all get together and mug Mother Teresa.

Rothmiller and others tried to hang on to their identities as cops. But there were always pressures from above, subtle and not so subtle, to turn them into intelligence operatives—night sleuths who watched everything, jotted it down, then silently passed it on to their masters.

And over and over, the gathering of this intelligence called for methods that strained the rules and uncovered relationships that defied Hoyle's rules. For example, OCID was tipped that a certain mob guy had moved to Southern California from the New York area. He happened to be the individual who "rolled" on the drug dealers *The French Connection* film was based on. In fact, the signature chase scene was patterned after an actual experience of this mobster-turned-informant.

Rothmiller drove over to the FBI's Orange County office in Santa Ana and discovered that this ex-New York gangster had been moved by the government under the auspices of its witness relocation program. He was now working as an assistant to a Newport Beach restaurateur. An FBI agent in the office produced a detailed notebook listing many of the relocated witnesses in Orange County, complete with photos, real names, criminal records, and federal case numbers.

Federal law dictated that among federal officers, only U.S. Marshals were authorized to have any contact with relocated witnesses. So arguably even the presence of such a notebook in the FBI office was unethical, life-threatening, and possibly illegal.

But the theory was, if this guy could provide information on wiseguys in New York, maybe he can dig up something for us in Southern California. As every smart cop knew, relocated mob guys didn't generally enroll in medical school or something at their new location. They continued working as crooks, only this time under federal protection. "We're not supposed to talk to him, but we are," the agent confirmed.

Rothmiller thanked the FBI agent and went to see the witness. After all, the laws proscribing the federal agencies from contacting the witness did not apply to local police. The man was surprised that an LAPD detective knew his real name, but he didn't panic. Clearly he was not eager for anyone to revive the New York mob's interest in him.

He admitted talking with the FBI, but he also contended he wasn't giving up much. He boasted that the agents were easy to fool. If he passed on righteous information, he protested, it would just put him in more danger. So he gave the agents "bullshit." For this, he was pulling in $1,500 a month over and above his stipend from the U.S. Marshal.

After this conversation, Rothmiller used this informant only as a way to evaluate the veracity of the FBI's information to him. Because the informant told him exactly what he had said to the FBI, it gave Rothmiller a perfect opportunity to gauge just what the FBI told him about what the agents thought they knew. Such were the ways of intelligence gathering among different, often feuding agencies.

Rothmiller even tried to warn the federal agents he had information that their informant was being less than candid with them, but they refused to believe the warning.

Meanwhile, this informant played so many ends against the middle he could have passed for a hairball. Eventually he entered into an affair with the wife of his restaurant employer. She dumped her husband, married her new boyfriend, and together the happy couple acquired two of her ex-husband's three restaurants in the divorce settlement.

Chief Daryl Gates once boasted that when he was OCID captain during the sixties, he took personal action when he heard that Sam Farkas, once an associate of mobster Mickey Cohen, was pressuring some people into joining a bookmaking operation. Farkas was then the successful operator of a carpet business on Wilshire Boulevard. Gates had Farkas picked up and brought to his office.

According to Gates, he told Farkas that if he didn't stop whatever it was he was doing, Gates would lean on him so hard that "not only would he be out of the bookmaking business, *all* of his businesses would end." And that was the end of that.

Although that might have sounded like a terrific scene for a cops-and-racketeers movie, the reality was, sometimes gangsters did in fact weary of the rackets and try to go straight. Aside from questions of propriety and the U.S. Constitution, particularly the Bill of Rights, what if Gates had proceeded to destroy Farkas? Furthermore, what if Gates's information were faulty?

Had Gates tried to charge him with a crime, Farkas would have had the benefit of trial by a jury of his peers. But what happened to his rights when there were no charges, no lawyers, no jury?

Driving a man out of his legitimate business because of a suspicion he might be up to something illegitimate was an oft-used OCID tactic that survived Gates's stewardship of the intelligence division. Lots of small-time hoodlums moved in and out of legitimate occupations all the time. When a gainfully employed Roger X proved to be a burr in the OCID saddle, a division detective would simply call on the individual's employer, flash his badge, and say, "Does Roger X work here?"

"Yes, why?"

"Well, he is currently under investigation for his involvement in organized crime."

So much for Roger X's gainful employment.

This was yet another variation of LAPD street justice.

Years later, a Dixie con artist would move to Southern California, and an OCID detective would learn he was setting up a brand-new business in the Orange County community of Fountain Valley. This man wasn't a fugitive, had been charged with absolutely nothing, and wasn't even planning to operate his business in the City or County of Los Angeles.

His new venture was a tanning salon. But this was only the late seventies, and no one in OCID had ever heard of a tanning salon. The guy was a con artist, according to his sheet, and sure enough, why would anybody actually pay for a suntan in Southern California? Must be some kind of scam.

In addition, this was contempt of cop—not only taking his con game into Southern California, but doing it openly, with a storefront sign, no less. This was taken as a challenge to the very manhood of OCID. An insult to the *cojones*. There were certain things you just didn't get away with around this neck of the beach, and it was time this cracker learned just what the hell they were.

It wasn't Rothmiller's case, but he accompanied another detective for a visit to this guy who was unintentionally waving a red flag at the unit. Like con artists everywhere, he was quite personable. Surrounded by an army of contractors and suppliers as he readied the place for business, he told the detectives exactly what he planned to do—open a place where people could buy a suntan.

Sure, they thought. And right away, OCID detectives alerted local authorities to the impending menace. Rothmiller, he is sad to have to admit, was among them. "This guy is about to *pull* something," Fountain Valley police were told. "You can do what you want, but we know what we'd do."

And that's what the Fountain Valley police did. They unleashed entire platoons of building and fire inspectors on the poor schnook. And the inspectors issued warnings like an avalanche of Wall Street confetti.

Rothmiller stopped in again. The man had opened the business, but the inspectors kept ordering him to tear everything apart and start all over again. He had no idea what was behind all this. "The fire department came in here yesterday," he complained, "and they said I have to put another ceiling sprinkler in that corner way over there. If I don't, they're going to pull my permit and close me down. It's gonna cost a fortune!"

Then there was the building inspector. "He stopped by this morning and said my wiring was not to code. I *know* it's to code. But the prick said I couldn't do business until it was redone."

The inspectors hammered on him like this for two months, day after day, until they drained his capital and he threw in the tanning towel.

A few years later, of course, tanning salons would proliferate all over the country, including Southern California. By this time Rothmiller and the other OCID men realized that their prey had just been trying to go straight. But they hadn't let him do it. Instead, they had punished him for the crime of premature business foresight.

It was yet another reminder that perhaps the Bill of Rights had a place in government after all.

· 8 ·

Palace Intrigues

Although the OCID captain and the political team reported directly to the chief of police, the department's chain of command was structured so that no part of the chain was neatly tied in place. There was supposed to be a checks-and-balances system always at work to prevent corruption. Vice and narcotics cases, for example, were investigated by vice and narcotics units within the geographical divisions and also by Administrative Vice and Administrative Narcotics, two centralized units that were supposed to be pursuing major cases. But these units were also supposed to be watching each other.

The checks-and-balances system had been set in place before Gates's time by his mentor, Chief William Parker, who had plucked Gates from obscurity and set him on the LAPD fast track. Designated as Parker's personal driver and all-around gofer, Gates learned police espionage at the feet of the master and later employed it as Parker's OCID commander. Under Gates's reign, LAPD units continued watching each other.

This internal scrutiny was supposed to be in the interest of keeping the department clean. And in fact, the kind of corruption seen in some other police departments around the country—cash-filled envelopes distributed around the department like chain letters—was not a part of the LAPD style. There was evidence some of this occurred, but it was not pervasive, and so the evidence was swept away to keep the department's reputation intact.

Meanwhile, the checks-and-balances system provided a built-in excuse for a subtler form of corruption that wasn't based on hinky finances. Instructed to keep an eye on one another, the top pogues had only to make a short leap in tactical strategy to employ espionage against their rivals in order to win some advantage within the department's internal rat race.

Sometimes the department, therefore, took on the character of a fifteenth-century Italian duchy; palace intrigues were everywhere—feuds that flared up and sputtered awhile only to flare up again as nobles and prelates fought for position.

As Rothmiller took his place in OCID, he was trying to figure out just whom he worked for. Although his captain reported directly to the chief, the assistant chief who headed the Office of Special Services was given the latitude to play a hand in OCID. From time to time orders were sent down that were said to come from this assistant chief, who wielded power of his own over the OCID palace guard.

Rothmiller was once ordered by an OCID lieutenant to quietly investigate a deputy chief of the department. "Has he been accused of anything?" Rothmiller asked his supervisor.

No, the lieutenant answered. He made it clear that Rothmiller was just supposed to look the guy over and see if he could find anything to keep him in line. This order, Rothmiller was told, had come from the target's rival, an assistant chief. It appeared to stem from just another one of the ongoing pogue territorial disputes. Rothmiller was sure that no OCID lieutenant would take it upon himself to investigate a deputy chief. Clearly the order came from above.

Rothmiller was also ordered to investigate a Los Angeles County official. One of the official's own intelligence officers told Rothmiller that periodically he was ordered to go over to Palm Springs to investigate personal real estate investments for his boss. Rothmiller passed this on and was congratulated. He had stockpiled potential ammunition for the LAPD honchos. You never knew.

When Sherman Block was elected Los Angeles County Sheriff, he became an investigative target. OCID kept updating intelligence files on the entire array of police executives from neighboring departments. This tendency to spy on friends and neighbors was a disease that seemed to have no cure. After Gates was named chief, Deputy Chief Robert Vernon, a losing finalist for the top job, had the temerity to order some of his people to investigate his boss.

Gates, who got wind of it, believed Vernon was trying to get something on him in hopes of replacing him. So Gates had Vernon investigated. For years rivals of Vernon had swiped at him by contending that his fundamentalist Christian views were affecting his personnel decisions. The two hard-nosed police plutocrats were departmental foes before and after Gates went past Vernon on the great pogue ladder.

Eventually, Vernon would sue the city, contending that its agents had improperly investigated his religious beliefs. This suit revealed more dirty LAPD linen. In a court declaration related to Vernon's suit, Detective Neil K. Spotts admitted that he headed up Gates's investigation of Vernon. Spotts was part of the two-man political team on OCID and therefore a key quiet team player. Eventually Spotts would leave the department to direct security for Playboy Enterprises.

Once again, OCID dodged a bullet. No one among the new media pressed to find out why an Organized Crime Intelligence Division detective would be detailed for this kind of dirty work. Perhaps reporters assumed Vernon's church was a crime syndicate.

Rothmiller didn't have to wonder how long OCID's mission had been so perverted. Even Chief Gates was known to brag about the unit's bravado methods. In the old days—going back to Prohibition and into the thirties and forties—the LAPD had been a typically corrupt urban police force, probably even more corrupt than most. The town was brimming with brothels and bookmakers while casino ships traversed the waters offshore.

"Law is where you buy it in this town," Raymond Chandler wrote of Los Angeles in the forties.

The intelligence division's precurser was the gang squad. During the thirties and forties its detectives were little more than leg-breakers for the L.A. mobs. The unit was filled with top-notch ass-kickers whose job was to turn back potential out-of-town rivals at the train station. The usual method was to take the out-of-towners into the men's room and beat them senseless. The LAPD signature to the beating came with a reverse head slam into a porcelain sink and a suggested change in itinerary. Word of these little touches circulated readily around the underworld, which was exactly what the cops intended. After the beatings, the detectives sometimes helped wipe the blood off their victims. After all, it was just business.

But of course some out-of-towners slipped past the greeting squad or toughed their way through some other way. Division lore had it that one racketeer who refused to turn around was taken out to the desert by cops who forced him to dig his own grave. Then just to make sure he understood their drift, they fired a round over his head. Standing in a pit surrounded by pitiless cops, he got the message. They could kill him anytime they wanted. After all, they were cops. They left him there, shaking but alive, the story goes.

Eventually the local mob payoffs stopped, but OCID never learned clean tactics. Even during Gates's OCID tenure in the sixties, when New York and Chicago hoodlums came to town looking to score, OCID knew ahead of time. "Before they could claim their luggage," Gates recalls, "we had LAPD officers out there to greet them. We said, 'You're not wanted here—get out. Go get your ticket and leave.' We literally put them on the next plane home."

Gates then noted wistfully that such tactics would not work during the nineties. "We would be hauled into federal court for violating somebody's civil rights."

The fact is, gangsters rarely scare so easily. They are not timid types. It's possible this is the story Gates's cops gave him: "We talked tough so they left." But if indeed cops succeeded in turning mobsters back at the airport, it's a safe bet their tactics were more like head slams into the porcelain than lectures on propriety.

Whatever the real story, there was more than a touch of xenophobia at work: We don't mind our own gangsters, it's those ethnic hoodlums from out of state we won't tolerate.

It was also part of division lore that intelligence detectives once picked up local mobster Mickey Cohen for questioning. While he was away, other OCID men proceeded to plant bugs in every room in his house. Cohen was put away in prison for the last time in 1962. While inside he was beaten almost to death by another inmate and left disabled for life.

OCID's intelligence files were inherited from the old gang unit and to some extent from the Public Disorder Intelligence Division, the LAPD division that eventually changed names and proved to have even more lives than an OCID file. The OCID files went all the way back to the thirties. For a while the plan was to let PDID handle the political intelligence, but the gang investigators had espionage expertise that was sorely needed for this sort of work, and so OCID, born in 1957, was drafted for political duties as well.

Although the LAPD has long boasted that its superefforts beat organized crime activity down to insignificant levels, that has never been the case. The in-town gangsters who hired LAPD cops as their goons were not insignificant. And some of the out-of-towners who pierced the porcelain welcome mat—men like Jimmy Fratianno of the Cosa Nostra and Benjamin Siegel of the Kosher Nostra —were certainly not insignificant either.

As Rothmiller became even more familiar with OCID files, he eventually concluded that OCID's tactics had in fact been toned down under Chief Gates. When his mentor Parker headed the LAPD during the fifties—actually from 1950 to 1966— the department's police spies barely bothered to cover its tracks. Those were the old Red Squad days. It was like a bull elephant swaggering through the forest, relying heavily on bugs, phone taps, and "black bag jobs"—actually breaking and entering in order to gather information. Yet during some of those years Gates headed OCID, so it appeared nobody had clean hands when it came to LAPD intelligence.

A series of politicians retreated from confrontations with the strong-willed, egotistical Parker, an unelected appointee who was clearly the most powerful politician in the city. In addition, Parker had the support of the Chandler family's *Los Angeles Times,* which in those years was almost a caricature of itself—a union-hating, red-busting, no-prisoners, monolithic media tyrant.

Then as later, during Gates's time as chief, intelligence was gathered on both friends and foes. Why friends? Because friends might not stay friends. But if they did, solid intelligence could be employed to help them out when danger lurked.

When George Deukmejian was making his soon-to-be successful run for governor in 1982, OCID discovered that the now-defunct Los Angeles *Herald Examiner* was sniffing around some of his campaign expenditures. Specifically, it appeared campaign coffers might have been used to install bulletproof glass in the candidate's Long Beach home and perhaps to make other improvements. That could prove embarrassing. It looked too much like ex-President Nixon's use of hundreds of thousands of dollars in taxpayer funds to improve his own homes in San Clemente, California, and Key Biscayne, Florida. The President's aides had also claimed the improvements were for security purposes.

A warning was passed to the Deukmejian people through the Long Beach Police Department intelligence unit. The Deukmejian people immediately passed a magic wand over the financing and then issued a press release to demonstrate just how aboveboard everything had been all along.

OCID's tactics were of course reversed for political foes. In some cases such people might get subtle warnings to change their ways. But others, like Mayor Bradley, were considered beyond threats, beyond redemption. Bradley and Gates were such bitter enemies that when the OCID got anything nasty on Bradley it would be put out there for all to see, and fast.

When OCID learned that Bradley had chartered a private jet from a certain local firm out of John Wayne Airport in Orange County, it was bingo at first sight. The company's owner was under federal investigation for reported organized crime involvement, as was his flight service. That might seem like a tenuous connection to the world of organized crime, but it was one of those associations that just didn't look good to voters. OCID leaked the story.

Bradley was not nearly careful enough for a man with such determined enemies. He no doubt felt somewhat invulnerable because he was virtually adored by the *Los Angeles Times,* which during the seventies had flopped its political allegiances from archconservative to big-business liberal.

Bradley, backed by the *Times* and other powerful interests with downtown real estate holdings, jammed through incentives for a tide of construction that changed the face of downtown L.A. No longer would Los Angeles be a collection of suburbs in search of a city. Under Bradley's tenure, Los Angeles built a high-rise skyline, much of it financed through Japanese capital.

But of course L.A., then as now, had almost no commuter alternatives beyond its tangled freeway system. And the rebuilding of downtown, by relocating tens of thousands of office workers from outlying areas to the steel towers in the central city, created arguably the worst day-to-day traffic mess in America.

Years later, when a *Times* reporter discovered

Bradley had a personally lucrative financial arrangement with two banks that were doing big business with the city, a *Times* editor killed the story. He said it needed more work, but he also failed to ask the reporter to do any more work on it. Nor did he say just what that work would have to consist of. This was in 1986, when Bradley was in the midst of making his second unsuccessful run for governor.

The dying *Herald Examiner* got wind of Bradley's shady dealings months later, after he had lost the statewide election. The paper ran a hard-hitting story right away. Suddenly the *Times* took an interest, too, and published virtually the same article that, before the election, it had deemed unworthy.

In the OCID, Democrats and liberals always drew more attention than conservatives and Republicans. Conservative dogma was more in tune with the accepted cop version of right and wrong as absolutes. Democrats were more apt to see victims and thugs as being tied together in a sometimes frantic, sometimes mournful socioeconomic dance, occasionally even changing roles or switching partners. This more cerebral approach by the liberals could make a cop's job even more difficult to handle emotionally. It was far easier to see good guys and bad guys, period.

Looking back at his tenure as chief, Gates declared that "conservative Republicans or Democrats tended to support the police department while those with liberal leanings instinctively viewed us with skepticism." Anyone looking at the direct attitudes and comments of the players would have to agree. But there were some liberals who argued that a longer view of the issue might show different results.

For example, liberals viewed gun sales to felons

and the mentally ill with a great deal of skepticism indeed, while conservatives looked upon the suggestion of waiting periods to check out potential buyers as an asault on the safety of honest citizens. This paradox was no better demonstrated than when conservative icon Ronald Reagan, the guns-for-everybody president, was shot down along with his press secretary on the streets of Washington by a mental patient who bought his weaponry over the counter from a gun shop.

Meanwhile, conservative forces were the bedrock of California's revolutionary Proposition 13 tax-cutting initiative. Its effects were to curtail spending across the board for public programs, including public safety.

After 1978, which was both the year of Proposition 13 and the year of Gates's ascendancy to chief, the state's revenue sharing with cities and counties began to evaporate fast. And Los Angeles, thanks at least partly to this monumental change in financing, maintained fewer cops on the street per capita than any large city in the United States. Even bankrupt New York City was better protected.

But the LAPD was more interested in its perceptions of how politicians stood in regard to its get-tough posture on the streets than how they lined up on other, perhaps more penetrating issues. Gates wanted the LAPD to stride the streets like a colossus. That's what really counted.

Bradley, in fact, opposed Prop. 13. But he was also a black, liberal Democrat, and, perhaps worst of all, only a lieutenant when he retired from the police department. Upper-echelon pogues shared a common loathing of the circumstances that had allowed this lowly black lieutenant to leapfrog over their stations in life. They outranked him, so they must be superior.

Meanwhile, the department struggled along with

two officers per thousand residents while most cities had approximately four. And the strapped LAPD continued throwing funds at its pervasive political espionage campaign. Whenever rumors of the political espionage surfaced, of course, the chief's office denied them. The local news media never gave them a serious look.

OCID was conducting massive operations against noncriminals for no other reason than to try to embarrass them or pressure them sometime in the future. Pickings were good.

But the OCID detectives were only the agents of discovery. Everyone was sure these nuggets were being used for political blackmail, but in political cases, they were not the ones to make the squeeze. This last step, the actual use of the material, was never trusted to the rank-and-file detectives. They were assigned to put the victims on the rack all right. But it was someone above them who turned the winch.

The way the OCID detectives pieced it together, the winch turner was someone who would make a mysterious appointment with the individual and then with a concerned expression say something like: "We really got lucky on this one. Somebody got ahold of these awful photos and we were able to intercept them. It'll be okay now. There's nothing to worry about."

Of course then the targeted somebody looking over the photos knew he had plenty to worry about indeed. He was now in the local Hoover file, and there he would stay. Even beyond his death.

Around election time, the political team would circulate among OCID detectives to remind them they were looking for information on the candidates. After Rothmiller teamed up with Skrah and began working criminal cases, these solicitations by the designated political spies would cause him less heartache. But then a pogue would pull him away from a real case to run a surveillance on a noncriminal heavy hitter and the irony of the situation would strike at him all the harder.

He was a cop. Why should he waste his time watching people who weren't suspected of committing any crimes?

• 9 •

Mob
Rule

A Chicago area cop joined the short list of cops from outside agencies whom Rothmiller trusted implicitly. The two cops often shared long-distance information on what the mob was up to. Increasingly the mob rackets spanned a geographical triangle that stretched from Chicago to L.A. and Las Vegas and back to Chicago.

While working with Rothmiller, the Chicago cop, who was part of a small but effective regional organized crime task force, scored a major triumph. The Chicago team was only a five-person operation but very savvy. The Chicago detective had earned the trust of a high-level mobster there who was feeding him excellent information. This was no ordinary soldier who saw only bits and pieces. He was an assistant capo working for Tony "the Ant" Spilotro, the Chicago mob's point man in Vegas.

If push came to shove, the mobster informant knew, it wouldn't hurt to have a friend in the Chicago Police Department. But of course he was also afraid for his life—and extremely careful how he played this game of crossed loyalties and dual conspiracies. He wouldn't talk to anyone but this one police lieutenant.

Even in the cruel company of the Chicago mob, Spilotro was a particularly feared man with a well-earned reputation as torturer and killer. It wasn't easy to convince anyone to cross him, particularly someone close enough to know just how true those tales of brutality were.

This mob lieutenant was the sort of informant Rothmiller dreamed about. So far it had been next to impossible to get good intelligence out of Las Vegas. For one thing, the local police department was considered a questionable source. One of its intelligence officers had even been caught in a hinky deal with Spilotro. The Law Enforcement Intelligence Units network thereupon suspended the Las Vegas intelligence unit.

But the Chicago task force wasn't asking the informant specific questions about Los Angeles, as Rothmiller would. If he could question this Spilotro lieutenant directly about the L.A.-Vegas mob connection, there could be a gold mine of intelligence. It would be like getting a KGB general to spill his guts.

He immediately started campaigning to get this guy to talk to him. Rothmiller didn't go around his Chicago cop friend, but rather tried to enlist his help. He went out of his way to gather up anything that might be of value to the Chicago task force. And he called up all his chits for past favors. He promised and cajoled his Chicago cop. "You've just got to help me out on this. I won't let you down," he said.

"Okay, I'll see what I can do," the detective finally answered. "But my guy's very skittish. We'll have to be careful."

And the Chicago cop worked hard to persuade

his housebroken mobster that he could trust Rothmiller as he trusted him. Keep your word to Rothmiller and he'll keep his word to you, the cop said. And it wouldn't hurt to have a friend on the LAPD. You never knew.

Finally Rothmiller heard those beautiful words: "Okay, it's all set," the Chicago cop said. "We'll fly him out to Vegas. You can meet him there and then the rest is up to you. He believes me that you're a good guy."

Joy of joys. Rothmiller was on a cloud. Naturally he would go to Vegas with his partner. That was standard police procedure for such an important meeting. It would provide backup physically, of course, but also two heads were better than one. Most important, the partner would be a witness. Sometimes bad guys met cops and then claimed afterward that the cop had taken a payoff.

Rothmiller told his LAPD lieutenant the good news and said he and his partner would be flying out to Vegas. The lieutenant told the captain.

"Fly out to Vegas?" the captain told Rothmiller. "Forget it."

At first Rothmiller didn't understand. "Forget what?" he said.

"Forget flying out to Vegas. I won't approve it."

"But why not?"

"If this guy wants to talk to us," the captain said, "he'll come here."

No, no, this couldn't be happening. Somehow Rothmiller had run into some pogue obstacle, an inexplicable speed bump of mindless sludge that could halt everything. Maybe he shouldn't have said "fly." Maybe the captain was worried about the money. Actually, OCID detectives were tight enough with Western Airlines to cadge a couple free seats anyway. There was always space on weekdays. But probably the captain didn't know that. In fact, the sheer tonnage of what this captain didn't know about police work could sink the *Bismarck.*

"We'll drive, then," Rothmiller found himself saying. "It'll cost us next to nothing, just gas. This Chicago task force hardly has any money. They're just a little outfit. But they're willing to pay for the flight to Las Vegas from Chicago. All we have to do is get the last two hundred and fifty miles. This guy could be the best informant we've ever had. Don't you see that?"

"If the guy's really serious about talking to us," the captain repeated, "he'll come to us."

It didn't make any sense. It was the mentality of a pogue. Maybe he even knew he was wrong. But once he announced his decision, he wouldn't back down. That might be construed as an admission of stupidity. With a pogue, no remained no.

"But this is no way to treat the guy," Rothmiller pleaded. "Is he supposed to fly here on his own money so he can do us a favor?" Rothmiller knew how these mob guys thought. Sometimes it was the money that counted. In this case it would be the insult that counted. The man would never stand for it.

"Tell him to take a Greyhound," the captain said. "That won't cost him much."

Rothmiller stared at the captain in disbelief. Nothing he said made any sense at all. It was like a bad dream—a bad dream about a bad police department.

There was no way Rothmiller could ask this Mafia lieutenant to cross the desert in a Greyhound bus like a slot player. And if Rothmiller wanted to prove he could be a powerful friend to this guy, asking him to take a bus to town was the worst way to do it. His cop connection in Chicago wouldn't carry the message anyway. He wasn't dumb. But he wasn't Rothmiller's captain, either. This pogue was.

There was nothing left to do. Rothmiller called his Chicago cop and canceled out.

"I don't believe it," his friend said. "What kind of fucking goofballs do you work for, anyway?"

"Don't ask," Rothmiller said. He remembered that awful day many times afterward. Something would come up, and he would yet again recall he could have had his own high-level informant inside the Spilotro mob. He knew that the secondhand intelligence he received through the Chicago task force wasn't 10 percent of what he might have had. And there was no telling where that connection could have led. It could have opened vistas of information he couldn't imagine, solved big crimes he didn't even know were being committed. The moral was clear: If you could avoid it, never tell a pogue what you're up to.

Afterward Rothmiller would watch entire teams of detectives head out to surveil some state legislator who hadn't been accused of anything. Then he would try to envision the captain's response had the informant been inside the staff of some liberal politician who'd been annoying the police department. It wouldn't be hard to predict: damn the torpedoes and full speed ahead.

Rothmiller had managed to carve out a specialty within the unit as a Mafia and narcotics specialist, but even so, he had already been ordered to collect information on such notables as Mayor Bradley; Democratic Congressmen Edward Roybal and Mervin Dymally of Los Angeles; L.A. City Councilman Richard Alatorre; State Senator Art Torres; Baltimore Colts owner Robert Ursay; Rams owner Georgia Frontiere; Chuck Knox, then coach of the Rams; and Hollywood mogul Dino De Laurentiis. None of them was accused of any crime. These were all fishing expeditions.

Everyone in OCID knew about a producer who,

tired of being hounded by division detectives, once tried to ram a surveillance car. The detectives skedaddled. The producer, whether he knew it or not, had found a perfect countertactic. OCID could not afford to get in such confrontations. They could bring media attention to a palace guard that required absolute silence in order to function the way the brass intended it to function.

More and more it appeared that the main reason Rothmiller's bosses even allowed him to specialize in criminal activities was so they might have contacts on that end of the investigation should they be lucky enough to discover that some notable became involved with the Mafia or narcotics.

By a freak circumstance, Rothmiller, while working as a community relations specialist, had found the lost toddler of future California State Treasurer Kathleen Brown Rice, the sister of the governor and the daughter of a former governor. The child had wandered down the street, and it was Rothmiller who took the toddler back to an immensely grateful mother.

When he mentioned the incident after he moved inside OCID, Rothmiller was thereafter hounded repeatedly by other OCID detectives who never tired of investigating the Brown family. "What can you tell us about them? What'd it look like inside the house? Anything weird going on?" Rothmiller would just reiterate that he barely knew Kathleen Brown Rice, but that she appeared to be a nice, perfectly normal person who was very thankful that her child was found unharmed.

Meanwhile, pogue tales floated around the division like old Looney Tunes cartoons. Old-timers still told the one about the time a squad of OCID detectives stuck a tail on Teamster boss Jimmy Hoffa after he landed at the airport. Hoffa got in a car and headed down the San Diego Freeway to San

Clemente, where he met with his ally President Nixon at the Western White House.

To set up a really good daylight tail without a helicopter required six to ten cars, and there were about that many teams on Hoffa. The cars took turns on point to avoid being spotted. From San Clemente, Hoffa's car headed east all the way to Las Vegas—a five-hour trip—with the OCID men discreetly behind him.

By the time they arrived in Las Vegas, the OCID men decided it was time to break off, and they made a deal with the Las Vegas police intelligence unit to take over. The lead investigator on the OCID team called the lieutenant back in Los Angeles to advise him they were all about to head back. Suddenly the captain got on the line.

"You guys are on your own time now," the captain told him. "Don't put in for overtime."

When the lead investigator hung up and told his men, they decided that the captain couldn't punish all of them. The team leader called back. "The guys got together and decided it's not fair for us to come back on our own time," he said.

"Well that's the way it is," the captain said.

"So we all decided if that's the way it is, we're going to leave all the cars here and fly home," the detective said.

The captain fumed awhile but finally relented. The men were not on their own time after all. It was a story told wistfully around the division—a comforting story about a pogue who lost an argument. There weren't enough of those.

After Rothmiller lost the battle to cultivate the mob informant, he plunged ahead with the informants he had. There was nothing else to do. He was upset, of course, but not enough to quit the division. Sure, he was working with pogues tied around his neck like quacking albatrosses, but he still liked the work. He still preferred chasing mobsters to hookers or joy riders. That's just the way it was, and there was no sense denying it.

Even as the other detectives in the division bitched about their plights, they knew they had a relatively good deal. If you were going to work in the LAPD, it didn't make sense to transfer. There wasn't any greener grass.

Among Rothmiller's list of informants was investigative reporter Bill Farr of the *Los Angeles Times*. He had briefly been a civil liberties hero during the seventies when, as a reporter on the Los Angeles *Herald Examiner,* a judge jailed him when he refused to reveal a confidential source.

Farr, who is now deceased, would pick up bits and pieces of information just like cops did, and trade them around for more. Meanwhile, he had his own list of informants who were in the underworld. It was a typical arrangement. He was one of the very few journalists who got to talk to an OCID detective. The LAPD was so secretive about the unit, it preferred the press would even forget it existed. And for the most part, it did.

Another unit, the LAPD's Press Relations Office, handled journalists and their problems pretty much the same way the Court Liaison Office handled judges. If a journalist was arrested for anything, say drunken driving, watch commanders were under standing orders to call the press relations people before booking. The reporter was then fresh meat, and the LAPD press team would decide just how to prepare it.

Although the LAPD held judges and journalists with about the same degree of contempt, the court liaison cops schmoozed the judges while the press relations cops weren't always so polite to journalists. OCID men looked upon the court liaison people as fellow intelligence operatives who worked a very specialized beat: they spied only on jurists.

Working within OCID, Rothmiller's network of contacts and informants seemed to expand geometrically. His unit affiliation gave him the standing to gather intelligence in places where many other detectives might not tread so readily. It was like having a great big set of extra sharp teeth.

He developed international contacts through Interpol, Scotland Yard, the Mexican Federales, Israel's Mossad, and the Costa Rican Federal Police. And he discovered that these international movers and shakers worked things just the way detectives did in the U.S. They had their shady informants; sometimes they protected them and sometimes they dumped them, given the proper enticement.

One day he might call the Mossad and ask a specialist on the Israeli Mafia for a rundown on a particular individual he suspected might have an Israeli police record. He would get an immediate response that was immensely helpful.

But he might make a similar inquiry to the same Mossad agent a week later on another individual and suddenly he would be ignored. If he were persistent, he might eventually hear something like, "We've been told that individual moved to France." Meanwhile, that particular individual was fencing hot jewelry from assorted Los Angeles motel rooms in Hollywood. But he was also, it appeared, someone who remained helpful to the Mossad from time to time.

The FBI would play exactly the same game. In fact, Rothmiller played exactly the same game. Everyone understood. The best source of information on criminals was other criminals.

Rothmiller had one informant who was particularly good at discovering the whereabouts of fugitives. Rothmiller would ask about a certain individual. "Give me a couple of days," his informant would say. And a couple days later he would give Rothmiller an exact address in Omaha or Louisville or someplace. It was uncanny.

One time Rothmiller asked his bloodhound about a burglar and forger wanted on a fugitive warrant. Sure enough, he came up with the address of a cabin at Big Bear Lake in the mountains ringing the Los Angeles basin. That was San Bernardino County, so Rothmiller called the information over to a San Bernardino sheriff's deputy he knew.

Next day Rothmiller received a call from the deputy. "Mike," he said, "I think you better drive up here."

"What's the trouble?"

"We found the guy all right, but you better come up and look this one over. When we popped him he had these documents with him. You better just come over and take a look."

When Rothmiller arrived at the sheriff's office the deputy showed him a very detailed plan to kidnap a Saudi prince for ransom. According to the seized documents, the prince would arrive in Los Angeles in a few weeks. It was a step-by-step plan that showed the prince's flight time, his Los Angeles hotel suite, the number in his entourage, his entire itinerary, everything.

The plan outlined how to get through the alarm systems, the equipment that would be needed, including Uzis, duct tape to gag the prince, and a specific medication to put him to sleep. Listed also were the precise tasks for each kidnapper. The caper required six to eight people. Nothing would be left to chance.

Maybe this little stinkbug of a felon just suffered from delusions of grandeur. But when he called the Saudi embassy, Rothmiller learned the Saudi prince was in fact arriving in Los Angeles on the indicated date. The embassy refused to release any information on the itinerary or divulge the name of the hotel.

And there was something else. The captured fugitive had two phone numbers in the documents. One was a Washington area number with a name and the initials *CIA*. The other was an international number next to a name and the word *Mossad*.

Rothmiller called the Washington number. It turned out to be an inside line that went straight into CIA headquarters. The man who answered was the same man listed on the document. Rothmiller had an Israeli operative check out the Mossad number. Same result. The name and number were accurate.

The jailed felon refused to give Rothmiller the time of day. Now what? Well, the Secret Service was charged with protecting potentates when they visited American shores. Rothmiller called the Los Angeles office, found the appropriate agent, and unloaded what he'd learned.

"We're awfully busy," the agent said. "Why don't you just drop all this stuff in the mail and we'll take a look at it if we get time?"

"Don't you even want to talk to this guy?" said Rothmiller, incredulous. "This is some serious stuff we're talking about here."

"No, we're just too busy right now. Just mail the stuff, and if we think there's anything to it, we'll call you back."

Rothmiller did what he was instructed, and the Secret Service never called back. There were some things you just never found out. He dropped the whole thing.

Rothmiller, who still had lots of bookmaking informants, received absolutely solid information that an assistant football coach at a large university in Southern California was sliding in bets for and against his own team, depending on his very inside information. Trouble was, there wasn't much percentage in trying to charge anyone with placing bets, even under these hinky circumstances. The law went after the bookie, not the customer.

Still, Rothmiller was outraged enough to call the headquarters of the National Collegiate Athletic Association. He found the appropriate person, who said, "To tell you the truth, we're not really interested. It goes on all the time."

A few years later, when Cincinnati Reds manager Pete Rose was caught in a betting scandal, it was never proved that he wagered on his own team, but he ended up going to jail anyway on a related charge. Rose should have coached college ball. It would have been safer.

As Rothmiller went over Sam Sarcinelli's telephone records, supplied by the FBI, he noticed that his favorite surveillance target had started making lots of calls to a specific New York City number. He checked a cross listing and got the name and address listed, and then he called the New York Police Department organized crime intelligence unit. A detective promised to look into it and call Rothmiller back.

Shortly afterward the New York detective called and asked for a secure mailing address that was in another state.

"Why? What's this all about?" Rothmiller asked him.

"Don't ask questions," the detective answered. He said he needed an absolutely reliable mail drop who would forward something to Rothmiller. Rothmiller said he would get back to him. He then checked with a trusted police friend in another state and told him the story, getting his cooperation in advance for whatever the New York detective had in mind.

"It's all set," Rothmiller told the New York detective. A few days later Rothmiller received an unmarked box in the mail, apparently mailed from New York via the mail drop. Inside were address books, photographs, slips of paper, and other odds and ends that looked like they came from someone's desk. In fact, it looked like someone had emptied a desk and thrown the contents in this box—the desk at the end of the Sarcinelli phone calls.

The New York detectives had pulled a black bag job for him, entering the premises and sending him whatever they thought he might be able to use. He looked through everything and then mailed it back to the New York detective without comment. Most departments made their own rules, and some rules were looser than others. No one Rothmiller knew in OCID would ever leave such an incriminating trail.

Then, tailing Sarcinelli one day, he watched the mobster pick up a man in the San Fernando Valley who had an amazing resemblance to the Colonel Sanders of fried chicken fame. The two men remained hooked up for two days as Rothmiller and other detectives tailed them from place to place. At the end of each day Sarcinelli dropped the Colonel clone off at a Woodland Hills motel. Rothmiller pulled the registration at the motel. The Colonel claimed a New York address.

Rothmiller called the NYPD organized crime unit and read off the name on the registration card.

"Oh you mean the Colonel," the New York detective said. "Is this a guy who looks exactly like Colonel Sanders?"

"Exactly," Rothmiller said.

"Yeah, he's big in the porno distribution business. He's hooked up to the Colombo Family. I'll get the file. Call me tomorrow and I'll have more for you."

Rothmiller did as he was instructed. But on his

second call, the detective sounded distant. The same man, but with a different manner entirely.

"What's the lowdown on Colonel Sanders?" Rothmiller said.

"I don't know what you're talking about," the detective replied.

Rothmiller checked. Was there some other detective in the same unit with the same name?

"No."

"But we just talked yesterday. You said you'd get the file on this guy." He read off the man's real name.

"It's all new to me," the detective said. "I'd love to help you if I could, but the name means nothing to me."

"But you said this guy looks like Colonel Sanders, remember? Exactly like Colonel Sanders. He's in the porno racket. Tied to the Colombos."

But it was no use. The detective was straining to get off the line. He didn't want to draw this out. Rothmiller let it go.

This didn't appear to be an ordinary case of protecting an informant. In those cases a cop never clammed up tight. He would just string the other cop along. Something like—sorry, that's all we have, I thought we had more information, but this is all there is.

Rothmiller concluded Colonel Sanders had a very special flag on his file that led to a payoff somewhere in the NYPD, making him an absolute no-no. Colonel Sanders? Never heard of him.

But other sources remained solid. Private security forces working for major corporations, for instance. These people were all former policemen, most of them retired. They were happy to cooperate just so they could behave like real policemen again. And they might need a favor sometime.

So detectives could pull someone's credit file and

find out who held his bank card accounts. Then it was a simple matter of calling that bank's security force to get copies of all expenditures. This was all privileged information, of course. But cops had their privileges, too.

IRS Intelligence was willing to provide copies of income tax forms, the same ones the government promised were absolutely privileged and would not be shown to anyone outside the IRS, so help them. Returns led straight to deals, properties, investments, a whole wealth of confidential data. And of course it didn't take much coaxing to get IRS just to audit the son of a bitch if he was guilty, say, of contempt of cop. IRS cops understood the rules. They were universal.

When several police agencies converged on poor Dominic Frontiere, husband of Rams owner Georgia Frontiere, it was the IRS that finally took him down. It was a silly bust, yet another example of the police hammering at some harmless individual who happened to be in the public eye while real criminals just couldn't get their attention. And OCID had much to do with it.

OCID, along with lots of other police agencies, figured, somehow, that the world of professional sports was a prime target for infiltration by organized crime figures, and so police targeted the teams for surveillance. Within its bowels there were OCID detectives who prided themselves on being sports-world experts. Among the places they would regularly hang out was Rams Park, the team's practice facility. There the investigators did nothing more than watch the daily comings and goings. They had no specific goal in mind, but merely added worthless scraps of information to the files of Rams' management personnel.

The Rams surveillance was so pervasive OCID half-expected to get caught. So it had already prepared a cover story. It seemed a South Pasadena bar and restaurant proprietor had wangled himself a volunteer position as the Rams' honorary equipment assistant. This meant he could stand around the bench at game time and hand out Gatorade. In his restaurant, a waitress had once been arrested as a bookmaker's runner. Through this tenuous connection, the Rams water boy and jock fetcher was perhaps placing the entire team in the ruthless grasp of the Mafia. That was the cover story, anyway. But OCID never had to use it. The Rams didn't seem to notice OCID detectives. They had other people to worry about, like the Bears and the 49ers for instance.

Among other agencies watching the Rams were the Orange County sheriff's intelligence unit (because the Rams were headquartered in their county) the FBI, the IRS, and the L.A. sheriff's intelligence unit. Sometimes there were enough operatives watching Rams Park to field a team of their own.

When the widowed Georgia Rosenbloom married Dominic Frontiere, the cops' suspicion fever rose into the red zone. To cops in intelligence, this was like mooning a flag-raising ceremony. They immediately increased surveillance. Why? First, sports owners were suspicious in general. Second, Georgia Frontiere was a former showbiz person. Third, her new husband was a composer, in showbiz as well. Fourth, he had an Italian name. Jackpot. And with all these agencies watching the Rams organization and calling each other back and forth to trade wisps of nothing, there was a sort of mob hysteria at work, much of it fueled by the ever-vigilant OCID.

After months, a sizeable Keystone Kops–style operation had nothing to show for itself but a big phone bill. Frontiere was legitimate. Eventually the investigators decided they ought to make some kind of arrest after all this anxiety. That's when the

IRS nailed poor Dominic Frontiere for scalping Rams tickets and not paying taxes on the proceeds. Players and front office personnel had been doing this all around the league for years.

It was like pulling over a motorist doing 65 on the Pasadena Freeway. Pick anyone you want. So they picked Frontiere. Vince Lombardi never knew how lucky he was he didn't coach in L.A.

Ironically, sometimes cops had trouble distinguishing organized crime from the Hollywood fantasies of organized crime—the godfather series, which portrayed Mafia dons as larger-than-life figures who commanded billions, secretly owned huge corporations, and directed giant armies of accountants, priests, and robo-warriors eager to fall on their stilettos for the don.

For years the OCID actually believed that Dominic Longo, owner of one of the most successful Toyota franchises in the world, must be a gangster. Cops who should have known better than average movie fans but didn't were convinced Longo's chain of dealerships must be a front for his real business: mob stuff. This would have been like Frank Sinatra using his fabulously lucrative show business career as a front for what was really important—taking bets on horses.

But dumb as the theory was, cops, particularly OCID cops, wasted thousands of man-hours surveilling the now-deceased Longo, who, like Sinatra, refused to let the cops tell him whom he could or could not rub shoulders with. And occasionally mob guys hung out at Longo parties, which was somehow supposed to justify all the police attention he received.

Longo, who knew a good joke when he saw one, decided to kill the cops with kindness. He offered cops and firefighters unbelievable car deals, and they poured into his dealerships like yahoos to a monster truck rally. Of course OCID detectives were ordered not to buy anything from Longo, but they routinely ignored the order. A good deal was still a good deal. So a detective who might buy a car from Longo on Monday could end up tailing him on Tuesday.

One day Rothmiller and his partner decided to do something that, at least according to Longo's immense OCID file, no one had ever done before. They went in and confronted him politely but directly to hear his side of the story. Ironically, the day they did so, there was a car full of L.A. County Sheriff's Department detectives sitting outside the dealership. Longo picked them out right away.

"They with you?" he said, smiling. "God, I've heard this stuff for a long time. Hey, I grew up with some of these guys. I give them jobs, but they're nothing jobs. One of the guys you're worried about, I pay him two hundred dollars a week to transport cars. He's a car runner. That's it."

Rothmiller and his partner knew exactly to whom he was referring—Jimmy Regace. They'd already wasted time checking him out. Regace lived in a miserable little Anaheim apartment in one of those smog-and-belch zones within coughing range of the Santa Ana Freeway. They had already concluded that if this guy were pulling capers, he wasn't very good at it. But the detectives' supervisors still insisted this hand-to-mouth prole was a Mafia don *craftily posing* as a car runner. Because that was the theory. Whether it was Longo or anybody else, any action undertaken by someone suspected of mob activity had to be a cover for something much bigger.

It was in keeping with this theory that a nameless OCID detective once turned in a report about an Italian named Albino Luciani. He had worldwide connections and had just assumed a position of even greater power in an organization that conducted immense money transfers, maintained a chain of wineries and other investments, and apparently paid little or no taxes on its immense holdings.

"The captain briefed the chief on it," a lieutenant told the detective. "Stay on this. They want to see more."

The detective smiled weakly as the lieutenant walked off. "Oh shit," he said to another detective who'd already read the report and laughed. It was a completely factual intelligence report, all right, but the subject's new name had been left off—Pope John Paul I. The pogues hadn't gotten the joke. Now what? Fortunately, they forgot about it.

· 10 ·

The Quiet Beach Team

After serving two years in OCID, Rothmiller spent several months on temporary assignment in Venice as a field sergeant. In the LAPD, it was unusual for a detective to also achieve the grade of sergeant, a position that had to be reached on a separate promotion track. Detectives were ranked Detective One, Detective Two, and Detective Three. By accepting the temporary station, Rothmiller received an extra gold star on his chart. He would thereafter be both a sergeant and a detective.

Working Venice would be a return to the grunt work of field policing. Instead of trying to outsmart mob schemers, he was out there supervising ordinary cops, attempting to put away rapists, burglars, muggers, and petty thieves. Venice was known for its pleasant beach and the zany characters who flocked to it—the magicians, the skaters and mimes, the mastodons of Muscle Beach. But not too many blocks inland were some of the toughest streets in Los Angeles.

Rothmiller knew it would be poor judgment to let his carefully built list of organized crime informants wither from lack of attention. So he led a double cop life, working the field in Venice, staying in touch with his network of informants, and filing intelligence reports on what he learned.

A field sergeant not only supervised the officers under him. Like a good NCO in the military, he was supposed to watch out for them. That was quite a job in Venice, because Rothmiller's lieutenant was an Internal Affairs Division alumnus who personified what IAD was known for around the department—destroying the innocent and blessing the guilty.

An officer who worked for Rothmiller was going to chiropractic school during his off-hours. When the lieutenant found out, he called in Rothmiller. "Did you know this guy was going to chiropractic school?"

"Sure," Rothmiller answered.

"Pull all his logs," the lieutenant said. "Then follow up on his entries and talk to everyone he spoke to. See if it's all proper."

This was a catch-all device used by pogues to drive someone from the department. Officers never kept their logs exactly as they should. They filled them in as they had time, and they summarized events, places, and times from memory. To pull an officer's logs and check each entry for precision against the individuals he interviewed in the field was just that same tired old tactic of nailing someone for doing 57 along the freeway.

"I don't get it," Rothmiller said. "What did he do?"

"If he's going to this chiropractic school," the lieutenant explained, "he's going to quit the department anyway. We might as well get rid of him now."

Rothmiller liked this particular officer. And he didn't see anything wrong with his preparing for a future outside the LAPD. In any case, this was too much to ask. Maybe he was a sergeant, but on this one he would stick to the code as though he were an ordinary officer: don't screw another cop. He refused to tear into the officer's logs. The lieutenant glared at him as though sizing him up for a noose. That was all.

Later the lieutenant discovered he had an officer who worked as a cement finisher during his off-hours. The lieutenant spotted the officer eating lunch at a diner the day after he had called in sick on the morning watch, which ended about four hours earlier. The officer said he was feeling better and would be in that night.

This time the lieutenant wanted Rothmiller to pull all the building permits within a 20-mile radius to see if the officer had been laying cement somewhere the previous day. He wanted him to call every concrete company in the area as well.

He wanted to see all the cop's business records and tax returns. He was talking about the sort of thorough investigation that cops should give to major felons but didn't because they claimed they were too shorthanded. Detectives didn't even show up at shooting scenes anymore unless someone was shot dead.

Fortunately, Rothmiller was leaving on vacation the next day, and under the rules, a complaint like the lieutenant's had to be investigated quickly or dropped.

When Rothmiller finally finished his Venice tour and returned to OCID, he felt like he'd just completed a voyage on His Majesty's *Bounty*. He was also welcomed back by a talented new partner, Ken Hamilton.

Back in OCID, he received a call from an Internal Affairs Division sergeant he knew. The sergeant happened to be an art connoisseur. He named an individual and asked Rothmiller if he'd heard anything about him.

"Every cop who's ever worked in the Valley knows him," Rothmiller said. "He's into everything—drugs, forgery, loan-sharking. You name a scam and he's worked it. What about him?"

"Well, he says he's got some Icarat sketches he might be willing to sell."

"I'd stay away from him," Rothmiller said. "Whatever he's doing, it's not straight. They're forgeries or they're hot or something. I'd really stay away from that guy."

"He seems like a pretty nice guy," the IAD man said. Rothmiller couldn't believe he was hearing this. This was a cop whose job it was to make sure all the other cops stayed clean. "Sure, he's a nice guy. All scam artists are nice guys," Rothmiller explained. "That's their business."

But the IAD sergeant again met with the scam artist, who offered him some authentic Louis Icarat ink sketches at excellent prices. The sergeant, not trying to hide anything, told Rothmiller he'd purchased two. If a cop engaged in such a questionable deal, he ought to be shrewd enough to be quiet about it. Rothmiller was sorry he knew anything about this, but he decided not to say anything.

Not long afterward, the art seller was busted for something, and of course he immediately rolled on the sergeant who'd bought his sketches. The sergeant had to turn them in, but he wasn't charged with possession of stolen property or punished by the department. Ignorance of the law is no excuse, though it was very questionable just how ignorant he was. But he pleaded idiocy and it worked.

Had this same IAD sergeant caught another cop

in the same circumstances, he no doubt would have nailed him to the station house door.

Rothmiller's favorite hobby, Sam Sarcinelli, created yet another lead. But this was one Rothmiller wasn't pleased to follow. While going over the phone logs with an FBI agent, he saw somebody at Sarcinelli's Sherman Oaks address had called an address near Laguna Beach that was listed in the name of California Attorney General John Van De Kamp.

Sarcinelli had lots of acquaintances in Laguna Beach, and Rothmiller figured it was probably just a wrong number, especially since the register showed the call lasted only a few seconds if any connection was made at all, which could not be determined for sure from the data. Rothmiller made this very clear in a verbal report.

Instantly his lieutenant asked for two conflicting written reports—one short and implying that in all likelihood this was just the case of a misdialed number, the other implying that this was no wrong number at all and that this could be an important intelligence breakthrough. With both reports in OCID hands, Rothmiller could eventually be blamed or commended, depending on which way the wind blew.

Sure enough, the information triggered yet another Keystone Kops–style chase of a politician. But not even Rothmiller could have predicted just how silly this one would get.

Chief Gates and Assistant Chief Ianonne of Special Services took turns going to a monthly luncheon of top law enforcement officers in California that was also attended by Van De Kamp. As it was told to Rothmiller by his captain, when the report was sent back up the line to Gates and Iannone, their reaction was: Hmm, we've been sitting next to this guy at lunch all these times and he never mentioned he had a beach house in Laguna Beach.

Laguna Beach is a pleasant artists' colony along Orange County's south coast that happens to be popular among gays, as it is among straights. But the brass put one and one together and to them, it added up to something suspicious. By not mentioning the beach house, Van De Kamp, it was concluded, was trying to hide something. *He must be gay*.

This called for some real police work! Rothmiller had caught this ball, and so he was told to run with it. Forget all that gangster stuff, man. Can't you see we may have caught ourselves a fruit? A liberal Democrat of a fruit, too.

The captain also advised Rothmiller that Gates and Ianonne felt besmirched, bothered, and bedeviled that, unbeknownst to them, they might have been sitting with a homosexual at all those brass-laden luncheons. It was a filthy betrayal all right, almost like they'd started to get somewhere with this gorgeous babe and then just at a critical moment, they reached over and . . . you know the story. They'd been fooled, or at least so they decided.

Actually, this particular beach house wasn't even in Laguna Beach. It was a few miles north and in fact closer to Corona Del Mar in the Newport Beach area than it was to Laguna. But that certainly wouldn't stand in the way of a good homophobic police theory about a married politician.

Also, it wasn't a house, either. It was a cottage on the beach that, Rothmiller found out, had been in the Van De Kamp family for years. He also learned that the utilities were listed under the names of Van De Kamp and another attorney—a corporate lawyer. To the brass, that clinched it: homo love nest.

Although Van De Kamp had not mentioned the

beach house to Gates and Ianonne, it was assumed there probably were lots of other things he hadn't mentioned to them as well. They probably didn't know what he thought about Sartre's *Being and Nothingness* either, but that didn't automatically mean he was a Hegel fan. "It's meaningless," Rothmiller tried to tell the captain.

Anyway, Rothmiller did what was expected of him when these things came up. He ran the name of the corporate attorney through the "fruit file" at the Rampart division. For as long as anyone could remember, that division was the keeper of the LAPD's files on lewd conduct. The lawyer came up clean. Lots of families held vacation cottages together on a private time-share basis, which would account for two names on the utility bills. Rothmiller turned in his conclusion: It didn't add up to much, and there was really no sense pursuing this any further.

But that wasn't the conclusion the pogues were looking for. They just had to find a queer Democrat. And so it came to pass that a quiet team was formed instantly. Rothmiller, an OCID lieutenant, and four other OCID detectives, including the two-man political team, were dispatched to a sandy beach well south of Los Angeles, where they set up a surveillance and even pulled in overtime money waiting for evidence of lewd acts within the Van De Kamp cottage. They didn't send six officers to serve homicide warrants.

"But we don't even know if he's down there," Rothmiller had tried to explain. "It's after Labor Day. He's probably up in Sacramento."

The pogues were hot for this and would not be deterred. When the surveillance team arrived, Rothmiller saw no signs of recent habitation. It was not a good beach day and there weren't many people around, making six detectives on a gay-sex stakeout that much easier to spot.

Two of the detectives were the only two black detectives in OCID. Two young black men hanging around south of Newport Beach stuck out like a couple of Oldsmobiles in Tokyo. It was a familiar problem. The racial dynamics of Southern California meant that black men were very much noticed in certain neighborhoods. And this neighborhood was definitely one of those neighborhoods. In fact, people were always calling the cops on the two black detectives from OCID. "There are two suspicious black men sitting in a car out here, officer. Could you send someone to check them out?"

Rothmiller finally walked up to the door and peered around. Absolutely no signs of life. A mass of cobwebs led from the door to the door frame. No one had been here in some time.

But back at OCID headquarters, the ball was rolling. A plan was already approved to rent a boat and watch the house from the beach side, where the stakeout might be less conspicuous. Besides, the theory went, people were less careful around the beachside windows. Maybe there would be more to see. The captain who approved the boat rental was the same captain who would not fly two detectives to Las Vegas to gather information for a lieutenant of Tony Spilotro.

When Rothmiller reported on the quiet team's first-day's findings to the eager pogues, he laid it out straight: "We're not going to come up with anything. The house is closed up. And we're going to get spotted for sure. I can guarantee it. Someone will call Newport Beach PD, and the surveillance will be blown. And if their intelligence guys find out that we were down there without telling them, there's no telling where the information might go. It could all explode in our faces, believe me. I want to make sure you remember I said this. You're taking a big risk. And it's just an empty house."

These words were unwelcome, but they had an

178

effect. The only thing OCID prized above political intelligence was the absolute secrecy that shrouded the gathering of that intelligence. How could the investigators do the things they did with TV cameras swarming around? It would be impossible. A story like this could land them on the editorial page of the *L.A. Times*. One wrong Conrad cartoon could finish you in this town. This time the pogues listened.

With much reluctance, they dropped the Van De Kamp surveillance. Later, Rothmiller learned that while OCID was trying to prove the attorney general was gay, the Public Disorder Intelligence Division had been trying to prove he was having an affair with a woman. Those guys came up empty, too.

On the eve of his departure from the LAPD, Gates published an autobiography. In defense of charges against his department, he wrote, "Everybody had read too many espionage stories. Images of police officers looking through a telescope, peeking into a bedroom window, following people, checking to see whom they met for political reasons, were conjured up by politicians and reported by the media. *None* of these things was being done, except as they had to do with our objective of moving in to thwart illegal acts disruptive of the public order."

Some OCID detectives contended there was a legitimate reason for some of their skulking around after the rich and famous. All sorts of criminal types tried to use celebrities and politicians. A good intelligence operation could warn, say, the local county commissioner that these particular individuals seeking his program endorsement were slimeballs. So somehow this made it all right to watch the rich and famous *for their own good*.

But neither Gates's explanation nor any other squared with reality. They were inventions devised after the fact, and the fact was, a secret police unit was operating, KGB style, in Southern California. There was no legitimate explanation for the Van De Kamp episode or the thousands of episodes like it. Of what crime was the Attorney General being accused? How was he threatening public disorder? And how many real crimes were committed in Los Angeles the day six investigators were ordered to spend that day hanging out on the beach miles beyond the city limit?

One day Fresno sheriff's deputies called. They were looking for a very dangerous fugitive they'd heard was on his way to Central America by way of Mexico. They believed he might be in a Mexican border town, but that was all they knew. The fugitive was a local police officer suspected of pulling a string of residential robberies with a gun and ski mask.

But Fresno deputies were not practiced in dealing with Mexican police, and somehow they'd learned OCID in Los Angeles might know how to proceed from there. The lieutenant handed this one to Rothmiller and his partner, who said they would make some calls. Of course they really didn't have much to go on. Mexico had lots of border towns. But Rothmiller called some federales he knew. Within twenty-four hours he received a call back. Their fugitive was staying at a hotel in Tijuana with a woman. They had him under surveillance.

That was some police work—for Mexico or for any other country. But Mexican detectives, working without sophisticated computer linkups or DNA fingerprinting or much else in the way of scientific gizmos, did things like that all the time. Rothmiller could give them the tiniest clues, and they'd solve the puzzle, fast. Rothmiller and his partner informed their lieutenant and went home for the weekend.

Next day their lieutenant called. Fresno, he said, was eager to take their man now. The deputies would charter an aircraft and take it to Brown Field in San Diego, just across the border from Tijuana. Would Rothmiller and his partner meet the lieutenant and the Fresno deputies at the border to facilitate the crossing?

This presented a problem. There was a time-honored system of handling these little de facto "extraditions" with the Mexican police—a swift, nonbureaucratic method that left little to chance. No paperwork, no lawyers, no mess. Mexican police would grab the fugitive, take him to the border, and simply order him to walk north. He had nothing else to do; he walked north.

At the U.S. end were border patrol agents primed for delivery. The fugitive walked into their arms, and lo and behold, they told the news media the next day, "We received a tip he'd be crossing." Well, it was sort of a tip. It was also sort of like walking the plank. Anyway, it always worked beautifully. There was also a variation on this procedure. Mexican police might take the fugitive to a predesignated hole in the fence and shove him through to waiting U.S. cops.

But these tactics—which were more or less an open secret among police agencies near the border —were never advertised to the press, the public, or departments as far north as Fresno. And they certainly weren't advertised to pogues. The "kick" just could not be done in front of someone like a pogue who might decide to use it later against the cop who arranged it.

"Our Mexican contact won't be available until Tuesday," Rothmiller's partner told the lieutenant. "But if you want to go down there now, we'll tell you who to contact in Tijuana."

That was fine with the lieutenant. He wanted to show these Fresno cops a thing or two. Rothmiller asked the Mexican police to snag the fugitive. They did. He would be waiting at the jail. Rothmiller forwarded the information to the lieutenant, who was delighted.

After meeting the Fresno cops at the border airport, the lieutenant drove an LAPD car to the Tijuana jail. There he became a bit pushy, the Mexicans explained later. They didn't like foreigners coming down and telling them what to do in their own country. The lieutenant wanted the Mexican police to accompany him to the border. The Mexicans were puzzled. This was no typical "kick." This L.A. lieutenant didn't seem to know what the hell he was doing and they didn't much like him anyway. They pulled the American fugitive out of his cell and marched him over to the lieutenant.

"We release this man," the comandante said. "You do with him whatever you wish. The lieutenant promptly snapped cuffs on the fugitive cop, who then refused to get in the patrol car. So, with several Mexican cops standing around watching, he shoved the fugitive into his trunk and drove off.

Upon reaching Brown Field, the lieutenant drove up to the Fresno deputies, opened the trunk, and handed them their fugitive, who of course began yelling "Kidnap!" The startled Fresno cops didn't know how these things were supposed to be handled, but they were certain this was not the way. Now it would be necessary to concoct a story and stick to it. Why didn't this idiot lieutenant at least have the brains to stick the guy in the front seat after he'd crossed over to the U.S. side so they wouldn't have to witness this?

But they wanted this man very badly. And they'd already come this far. They shut their eyes, threw him in the plane, and took off.

Rothmiller and his partner returned to work Monday. The Fresno police called the lieutenant.

Their fugitive, they said, must have had several thousand dollars in the hotel room, along with possible evidence from the robberies, such as clothing his victims might recognize, or even the ski mask. Where was everything?

"Any cash he might have had," Rothmiller explained, "well, the Mexican cops will consider that a tip. Forget it. But you might get the other stuff."

The lieutenant called Tijuana. Sure enough. No money was found, but there were clothes and other things.

There is a vital principal in criminal law known as the continuity of evidence. Physical evidence, to be used in a courtroom, must always be accounted for. It must be signed for as it is passed carefully from one police entity to another so there can be no accusations of tampering.

The lieutenant obtained the fugitive's belongings, rooted through them in his office, and sent them to Fresno in a box on a Greyhound. He signed nothing. The continuity of evidence was now as sound as a 99¢ watch.

Fortunately, there were plenty of witnesses to identify and convict the Fresno defendant without the physical evidence that was now tainted beyond recovery. But the next time the Fresno County sheriff's deputies needed help with a problem, they were not likely to call OCID.

· 11 ·

"Audience" with the Chief

OCID detectives met once a month, always on a Monday morning. The captain liked these meetings. But even monthly meetings were too much for the detectives. They hated them. Once a month for no good reason they would have to join the torpid flow of rolling metal boxes into the downtown maw with all the other high-rise office saps. The meetings were held either at division headquarters or the police academy near Dodger Stadium, in which case it was made a breakfast event. Both locations were nearly impossible to reach on a Monday morning. Many detectives drove two hours or more to get there. They were so infuriated by the useless bumper-to-bumper crawl that many of them made it a point not to do any work for the rest of the meeting day.

Just about everything said at the meeting could have been distributed in mailbox memos: You guys have to remember to use 2.5 lead pencils on those reports; You're using too much gasoline in division cars, so review your driving habits; that sort of

184

thing. But pogues seemed to enjoy the ritual of these announcements. They evidently roused primal memories of their forebears, who no doubt caucused with the dinosaurs.

Once, Rothmiller was asked to provide a rundown on the disposition of the Sarcinelli investigation. When he was finished, a couple of old-timers took him aside. Take it easy on this, they said. Try going a little slower. You're making the rest of us . . . well, you know . . . look bad.

One day a newly transferred detective spoke up at a Monday meeting. He noticed that this division held no training exercises. "Why don't we train on vehicle surveillances once a week?" he said. "We could take turns tailing each other and see how we do."

Several detectives looked at each other in pain: Where did they find this idiot brown-nosing son of a bitch? But then the captain spoke up, and sure enough, he was receptive to the idea. He probably figured that establishing a new training procedure might be a feather in his cap. "Well, what do you think?" he said. "Any other thoughts on this?"

Rothmiller raised his hand. "Do you mean like a realtor caravan?" When the laughter died down, he said, "The whole point of a surveillance is to follow someone without being noticed. If we just follow each other around, and the guy we're following knows we're following him, it would be like driving school or something. There's no point."

But he could see the captain might order the surveillance exercises anyway, just to show what an obstinate pogue he was. So Rothmiller tried another tack. "If you actually want a surveillance exercise," he suggested, "why don't we take a name out of the files we haven't worked in a while and see what he's up to? That way we might come up with something instead of just driving around looking at each other."

Then Skrah raised his hand and cut to the meat of the matter. The whole idea of grown detectives following each other around on the street was incredibly stupid, he said, and everyone ought to see just what a ridiculous waste of manpower it would be. He addressed the captain directly: "I'm surprised you'd even consider such a dumb idea."

That killed the discussion. After the meeting the captain called Rothmiller in and chewed him out for attacking him in an open forum. "But you asked for critiques," Rothmiller reminded him. But the captain had the last word. After all, he was the captain.

It was about this time that Rothmiller made an arrest—momentous occasion in OCID. Two informants told the fire department's Arson Squad about a hairdresser who was looking for a hit man. OCID was handed the case. It sounded weird, but posing as lowlife Mike Lange, Rothmiller showed up for an introduction.

It turned out that the hairdresser was deadly serious. He and his gay lover, another hairdresser, had quarreled, and he was still in the will. They owned a downtown beauty salon together. This screwball decided he wanted to take out his lover, take all the money, and get out of the business, too, which was another of his dreams. He'd decided to do this by blowing up the shop with his partner in it. "But we've got to make it look like an accident," he said.

"When you blow things up, it doesn't look much like an accident," Rothmiller explained.

"Yeah, but what if you blew up the whole goddamn block?" the hairdresser said. "That would do it. No one would blame me for that. They'd never figure it out. I'd be in the clear."

This deranged coiffeur, who was completely comfortable with the idea of exploding a downtown block and everyone in it so he could make a few bucks and show that he was no hairdresser to be trifled with, offered to pay the sum of $5,000 to get it done. Of course he would never find enough explosives to do the job for ten times $5,000. But he no doubt was a trusting victim of much prime-time television.

His fantasy was laughable in one sense, but he was in fact trying to arrange a murder. Lunatics like this were dangerous. This particular lunatic, Rothmiller's informants told him, never went anywhere without a pistol. The guy was always packing and he was the nervous type. And now he was telling Rothmiller to blow up a whole lot of people. Society would be much safer with this guy put away somewhere quiet.

Rothmiller arranged another meeting at the downtown Greyhound station. He told the hairdresser to bring $500—down payment for the destruction of one city block. That's when he would bust him. And yes, when he made his report, this time the pogues said he could make an arrest. Maybe it was true; at least they wouldn't let people get away with murder.

SWAT was called in to work backup on this one, which worried Rothmiller a great deal. As always, he was more afraid of being shot by a cop than by a crook. In addition, he was working with the Arson Squad, which specialized in discovering the sources of fires, not closing in on lunatic hairdressers. Naturally, that night, there were lots of mixed signals between the disparate authorities—and screwups.

But eventually Rothmiller caught up with the hairdresser outside a restaurant and informed him he was under arrest. Sure enough, the beautician reached for his pistol. But Rothmiller already had his pistol in the hairdresser's face. It was a screwball arrest, but it felt awfully good. Best of all, SWAT didn't shoot Rothmiller.

Rothmiller made one other arrest during his five years' service as an OCID detective: he caught a thief making a snatch in an auto parts store. Of course he set up arrests for other agencies and other LAPD divisions—almost always clandestinely, to keep the pogues off his back. But it wasn't the same.

One day a solid DEA agent from Chicago called Rothmiller. He was excited. "Sarcinelli just took off from here with some people in his Learjet, and according to an absolutely reliable source, they're transporting 100 pounds of cocaine. They're headed your way."

Knowing OCID would not cooperate in a bust, Rothmiller quickly reached a deputy district attorney he'd worked with. He was in the Organized Crime and Major Narcotics Unit. There wasn't much time. The plane would be flying into Van Nuys, in the San Fernando Valley.

Talking it over, they both decided that P.C. (probable cause) might be questionable for prosecution purposes. But 100 pounds of cocaine was just too big a load. They couldn't let it go by. They would have to stop and search and worry about the rest later. Even if an overly careful judge were to spring Sarcinelli, at least he wouldn't give him back his cocaine.

Someone else would have to be there to sign off on the bust or the OCID pogues would hang him out to dry, so Rothmiller asked Administrative Narcotics for help. But it was Friday afternoon already. And late Friday afternoon, Administrative Narcotics was not excited about 100 pounds of cocaine. The detectives there were starting their weekend.

Rothmiller and his partner started heading for the Valley, and of course traffic was dreadful. Friday afternoon in L.A. On the Valley frequency they requested help and a couple patrol officers in a black-and-white car were assigned to meet them. The patrol officers weren't sure how to handle it, but at least their hearts were in the right place.

"Just get them on a traffic violation when they're in the car," Rothmiller said. That's what the deputy district attorney had advised. The traffic violation would have to serve as probable cause for a vehicle search. That stood a better chance in court than searching the plane on the basis of a tip from an informant they didn't know.

Rothmiller switched to the OCID frequency, trying to get more help from the division. Four police officers would be a thin blue line indeed. They didn't know how many guns or gunmen Sarcinelli might bring to the dance.

Meanwhile, an OCID lieutenant listened in. Furious, he barked to Rothmiller: "Don't stop that car. What the hell's your P.C.?"

Rothmiller didn't reply. He wasn't going to let 100 pounds of cocaine hit the streets of L.A. just because his bosses were insane or idiots or both. The lieutenant didn't know whether there was probable cause or not. He just gave the order: no arrests. The ultimate OCID pogue, he said not to do anything until he got there. He was on his way to the Van Nuys airport—at least a forty-five-minute drive. It didn't sound like he was coming to help.

Before the lieutenant arrived, the plane landed with four passengers plus the pilot and copilot. The luggage was transferred to a waiting Lincoln and the two patrol cops pulled it over for failing to signal while changing lanes. Rothmiller and his partner waited nearby just in case. Rothmiller preferred not to be spotted by Sarcinelli, who had never seen nor talked to the nemesis he didn't even know he had.

The lieutenant showed up, and while he yelled at Rothmiller, the two patrol cops did their job. But there was no cocaine. They found some hashish residue in a pipe in the luggage of one passenger, but they didn't bother to try booking him. The Lincoln went on its way.

Rothmiller learned later that the plane had made a stop in Denver. The DEA agent in Chicago tracked it, but by the time Denver agents got there, everyone was gone. Either the cocaine was unloaded in Denver or the tip was bogus. But the Friday afternoon nervous breakdown boogie turned up some valuable intelligence after all. The passenger with the hash residue in his pipe was a Sarcinelli cohort named Lawrence Brady—who happened to be a Chicago policeman. After he got home, Brady was arrested for possession of seven pounds of cocaine in a gym bag. He resigned. But Rothmiller would have to wait for another day or another way to pull down Sarcinelli.

Meanwhile, he had to endure the rantings of an enraged lieutenant. "But I'm a cop. I'm supposed to be enforcing the law," Rothmiller said. "Why can't I make an arrest?"

"What kind of question is that?" the lieutenant said. There it was. When it came to arrests, OCID had an odd way of twisting situations into tangled coils of lost purpose and reverse response. An obvious reality was labeled foolish and the irrational earned accolades, became molded into the standard pattern. It was a kind of blue brain rinse.

Sometimes it was difficult to tell whether the OCID pogues could tell the difference anymore between truth and reality or whether they had gone past the point where they could make the distinction.

And then Rothmiller, still trashing Sarcinelli religiously, discovered his favorite mobster was involved in another scam. With some cohorts he'd formed a company in Long Beach. Rothmiller checked into it. The company sold a bogus contraption motorists were supposed to hook to the fuel line to improve their gas mileage by 30 percent. One scheme was never enough for Sarcinelli.

Rothmiller found a slip of paper that told him Sarcinelli planned to call Chairman Lee Iacocca of the Chrysler Corporation. The plan was to lure car industry icon Iacocca to a handicapped children's benefit so the cons could snap a photo shaking hands with Sarcinelli. They then would use the photograph to help market their useless gadget. The Sarcinelli team hoped to sell a few million contraptions quickly, then make the company disappear.

Also on the note was a phone number that was a direct connection into Chrysler. Rothmiller presented his findings to his captain. "We'd better warn Iacocca," Rothmiller said. He figured he might enlist Iacocca's help to round up the crooks.

The captain thought over this information carefully, then said, "You're assuming that Iacocca doesn't know what's going on. You know, Iacocca is an Italian, and there's a strong possibility he's involved."

Here was an epiphany, a perfect metaphor for OCID operations that went beyond the stupid attitude toward Italian-Americans. The intelligence division, which claimed it watched celebrities to protect them from bad guys, actually watched celebrities *hoping* they'd get mixed up with bad guys in order to control the celebrities. And it had no interest in bringing the bad guys to justice.

So Rothmiller didn't contact Iacocca, but evidently Iacocca, an engineer by training, didn't fall for any part of the Sarcinelli scheme. He never showed up to any bogus event or endorsed any bogus gas-saving item, and so OCID couldn't dig up dirt on the Chrysler chairman. Later, Sarcinelli and his people targeted Richard Flamson, then Security Pacific Bank board chairman. Without informing his superiors, this time Rothmiller warned the target.

Another Friday afternoon after a tough week. This time it was early in the afternoon. Rothmiller and Skrah were sliding out to beat the freeway madness that kicked off each weekend in the automobile jungle of the Los Angeles Basin. Almost home, they got a radio message to telephone OCID immediately.

"When can you get to P.C.?" asked the captain, meaning Parker Center police headquarters downtown. "You've got to brief the chief," meaning Daryl Gates. The captain's voice sounded tremulous. He was clearly unstrung from the prospect of this meeting he hadn't prepared for. Rothmiller and Skrah were a bit unstrung by the prospect of turning back and heading straight into the center of the city—a mad errand on a Friday. "What's he want?"

"He wants to know about organized crime influence in the garment district," the captain said.

Could he wait until tomorrow by any chance?

"Absolutely not. Can't wait," the captain said. "How long will it take you to get here? Fifteen minutes?"

Well, a little longer than that.

"Just get here!" Bang.

News hounds had been sniffing around the garment industry of late. A recent local television series was exploring the use and abuse of undocumented workers—most of them Mexican—in local sweatshops. As the TV journalists looked into this question, they began to pick up rumors of mob influence in the industry.

Skrah was considered the foremost expert on

192

organized crime within the L.A. garment industry. The central shrine of this industry was a high-rise structure along the edge of downtown that was known as the Cal-Mart. There, a maze of office cubicles and showrooms housed countless garment manufacturers. Most of the really powerful organized crime figures on the West Coast happened to maintain Cal Mart offices sprinkled among the others like dandelions in the petunias. Skrah had informants among both dandelions and petunias.

The garment business provided mobsters with the perfect front for moving large sums of money from country to country without the necessity of maintaining a large warehouse, office, or shipping facility. A garment firm office also didn't need to generate much activity to appear legitimate. Meanwhile, genuine manufacturers sometimes needed to borrow capital in a hurry to keep their lines afloat. The money sometimes came from loan sharks down the hall. It had been that way for a long time. The two OCID detectives sighed and headed into the heart of the L.A. traffic beast to review all this with the chief.

There to greet them was the OCID captain. "Now guys," he said, "there are some things to remember when you have an audience with the chief."

An hour of freeway traffic had not sweetened Rothmiller's mood. "Audience!" he said. "What are we doing—meeting the fucking Pope?"

There, at the gates of the temple of poguedom, the captain would not be baited into quarrels. "Don't sit down until the chief is seated," he lectured, and the three of them went in. The chief came in quickly and sat down, so the others did too, around a large, oval conference table. The room was quietly upscale, contemporary, dominated by a freestanding glass cabinet filled with swords, plaques, and other symbols of power. Also at the meeting was Assistant Chief Ianonne of Special Services.

A waiter came over. "Anything to drink?" he said. "Soda, coffee, anything?"

Someone ordered a coffee, cream, and sugar.

"Yes sir, very good," the waiter answered and went off to prepare and fetch it. Rothmiller wondered how Gates could defend keeping a waiter on his payroll. Then when the waiter returned, Rothmiller noticed the waiter's I.D. tag. The waiter was a commander, an exalted rank above captain. Suddenly Rothmiller had a vision of Gates years ago, when it had been his turn to carry in coffee, doing so for his mentor and kahuna Chief William Parker.

While Rothmiller was lost in this pleasing reverie, his partner Skrah laid out a detailed verbal flow chart of just how organized crime used the garment business as an effective front for so many of its schemes. In an hour's time he named names, places, methods, dates, and a few dead bodies. It was an effortless summary and had to be an education even to anyone with expertise in the field.

"They have been there forever and will most likely be there forever," he concluded.

"Hmmm," said Gates.

"Hmmm," said the assistant chief, who then said, "No, we can't really say that."

"No," agreed Gates.

"Yep," answered the assistant chief.

"Thank you, gentlemen," the chief said. Handshakes all around, the audience was finished.

In the hallway, the captain complimented Skrah. "But you kind of emphasized that there was a lot of organized crime. We don't really want to do that."

The LAPD had said for years that it was successfully *fighting like hell* against organized crime.

Thanks to its vigilance, there practically wasn't any, not in L.A.

Next day, primed with acres of new knowledge from the talk by Skrah, Gates could be seen in a TV sound bite giving his assessment of organized crime in the local garment industry. There wasn't any, the briefed chief said. Sure, there *used* to be, but thanks to this fine department, it had been cleaned out years ago.

· 12 ·

Easy Money Along the Border

Through an informant, Rothmiller and his partner Ken Hamilton found out about a used-aircraft dealer in Tucson who might be able to help them get the goods on drug smugglers. When they spoke to him, he seemed genuine, said he would like to help but didn't want anyone to know he was talking to the cops. How should they disguise their occupations? Around his office at the Tucson airport, he said, they would attract the least notice if they posed as drug smugglers.

When they checked him out, it appeared the plane dealer was in fact just an honest citizen trying to help stem the dope trade. So Rothmiller and Hamilton flew to Tucson undercover, in their sleazeball roles.

They wore concealed weapons and fake Rolexes. They clanked with gold and carried aluminum Haliburton briefcases that were all the rage in the dope trade that season. Smugglers thought drug-sniffing dogs couldn't smell contents through the aluminum (they were wrong).

Their Tucson informant worked out of a busy, well-staffed office, where he bought and sold a lot of old multiengine prop planes: DC-3s, DC-4s, and similar workhorses. Business boomed for aging aircraft that were cheap and dependable, could hold a lot of smuggled cargo, and could operate on short, unimproved runways.

In previous times smugglers operating such planes would run guns or just noncontroversial merchandise like TV sets from country to country in Latin America, avoiding duty payments. There was still a good deal of gun running going on, the aircraft dealer said. But more and more, the old prop jobs were being bought up by drug smugglers.

The Tucson businessman used to run guns for the CIA in Africa, and he was not easily shocked by the follies of mankind. But he didn't like this burgeoning drug trade. Down here along the border, he saw more and more legitimate and semilegitimate people going for the big narcotics score. And he said he wanted to help put a damper on it.

As he ran down the details for them, he pointed to a hangar complex about 500 yards across the tarmac. "See those guys over there?" he said. "That's a CIA operation. They're running all sorts of stuff into Central America through here."

As he further penetrated the smuggling racket, Rothmiller would pick up more and more references to arms shipments, the CIA, and Central America. He made references to all in his intelligence reports.

"Want to have some fun?" the aircraft dealer said. "Start walking over there. You cross that line and people will come out of that building. I guarantee it."

Rothmiller and Hamilton tried it. Just as they stepped across a painted line on the tarmac, two men, as though summoned by Pavlov's bells, came out of the building and approached them. "Can I help you?" one of them said.

Rothmiller said they were just visiting an associate across the way and that they were looking around. The two men stayed with them, saying nothing. They didn't leave until the two detectives stepped back across the line.

Later, the detectives and their informant took off in a car to go to dinner. Two surveillance teams in unmarked cars pulled out after them. After a few blocks, there were at least four surveillance cars on their tail. Rothmiller and Hamilton figured them to be local Tucson police. But the L.A. cops couldn't identify themselves. It would blow their informant's cover.

So the teams stayed with them all the way to a Mexican restaurant. When the detectives and the plane dealer sat down, two tails took a table nearby to try to pick up the conversation. None of this was terribly difficult for Rothmiller and Hamilton to spot. They'd been at the other end of these surveillances enough times. Still, it was an odd feeling to be watching from the targeted end.

The two detectives stayed in Tucson a day and a half, and they were surveilled the entire time. Meanwhile, their informant gave them a fine education. As an experienced gun runner, he proved to be an invaluable reference. Because gun and drug smuggling were done the same way, they had become overlapping businesses. In many instances the same individuals did both. They would send guns south, drugs north. No sense dead-heading when there was round-trip cash to be made.

Along with their education, Rothmiller and Hamilton put together a list of names. They heard savvy, verbal dossiers for each individual, each enterprise. The aircraft dealer had the details and he was also quick to admit what he didn't know, making him an even more credible source.

While they were in his office, a man who claimed to be a Colombian air force colonel came in to arrange some plane purchases. He appeared quite comfortable in the company of two men who appeared to be drug smugglers.

Later, when they were back in L.A., an idea came to Rothmiller. It was an idea that related in principle to those nondeaf-mute cards he had printed up when he was working vice.

Their Tucson source had showed them copies of a periodical called *Trade-A-Plane*. It listed classified ads for planes, pilots, and equipment. Lots of smugglers found what they were looking for through *Trade-A-Plane,* the plane dealer said. Why not place an ad and see what happens?

It was an idea he knew wouldn't sit comfortably with the pogues, so he ran the ad without asking them. It was chock-full of smuggler code words: "Multi-Engine Pilots Wanted. High Pay, High Risk, Spanish Speaking Desirable. DC-3 Experience Preferable. Resume to Agouti Corp." Then a box number was listed. Rothmiller paid for the ad and the postal box from the same OCID fund that was used to reward informants. "Agouti" was the name of a Latin American rodent.

The wait wasn't long. The ad brought in approximately 1,000 responses. They ran the gamut from a priest to about two dozen active law enforcement officers, federal and local, from all over the country. Two were from the LAPD. There were retired military pilots, retired airline pilots, all sorts of legitimate people. There were serious bona fide resumes and off-the-wall crazed scribbles from Lee Harvey Oswald types.

These last applicants included goofballs who couldn't fly planes but tried to sign on as enforcers. They bragged of weapons proficiency and contacts where they could obtain weapon silencers. There were pilots who hinted of smuggling experience and pilots who flatly boasted of smuggling experience. There was much more than Rothmiller expected. Clearly there was a kind of magnetic attraction at work here that prompted even genuine citizens to drop all the pretense of legitimacy. They wanted high pay for high risk and they weren't careful about what they had to do to get it. America's insatiable craving for narcotics was entering a new, intensified phase of addiction and corruption.

Now Rothmiller had to figure out what to do with this stuff. He began putting together an elaborate intelligence sting. From a trusted acquaintance who ran the Huntington Beach Inn, he arranged a free interview room. Then he tried to screen out all applications from people who might be naive enough to think this was a legitimate enterprise. Next, to be humane, he tossed out everyone outside a 300-mile radius. That way if an honest job seeker slipped through the first net, at least he wouldn't come all the way from Providence, Rhode Island, for nothing.

Next, he screened out all the cops. It wasn't likely any of these brazen cop applicants were working to gather intelligence against smugglers, because if they were, they wouldn't admit they were cops. They would assume other identities. But if cops came in and turned out in fact to be dirty, their respective Internal Affairs divisions would expect to pounce on them immediately. That would blow the sting. None of the discarded applications were thrown out. They were just set aside to be investigated at a more propitious time.

Next, there had to be a method to head off noncrooked undercover cops from other agencies. Sure enough, several police agencies asked the state's Department of Motor Vehicles for information on the Mike Lange whose name was on the mailbox rental. Lange had been listed for years in DMV files under a phantom Hollywood address.

These police inquiries to the DMV were all flagged. Such good-cop inquiries came in from the Orange County Sheriff's Office, the DEA, and a smattering of municipal departments.

Now it was time to deal with the remaining pile of applications. Rothmiller contacted the most flagrant-looking and the most promising in terms of being information sources. He set up appointments with about twenty-five applicants from 6 to 10 P.M. over three nights at the motel in Huntington Beach.

The next step was to make sure he didn't get killed by any of the applicants. As always, he was more afraid of getting shot by trigger-happy cops than crooks. Undercover cops might get through the application process somehow. This sting would require some manpower. He enlisted recruits from both OCID and Administrative Narcotics—all experienced undercover men.

And here at last was a perfect assignment for the two black OCID detectives. Yes, they had trouble passing in some undercover work, but when they took on parts as thugs in a dope-smuggling operation, they were immediate hits with everyone they encountered. Hispanic cops were also recruited, as were Anglos. There were about a dozen cops altogether. They wore flashy jewelry and bad attitudes.

Each applicant was told to ask for Lange at the desk. When he did, the clerk called the room and two "thugs" came downstairs to take him aside, pat him down, and escort him to the second-floor room. "Sorry, you understand. We have to look you over before you see Mr. Lange." Meanwhile, two undercover cops sat in the lobby. Two more were in the parking lot, and two more standing on the balcony outside the motel room.

As soon as the applicant went upstairs, the parking lot cops, watching for signals from the lobby cops, went through his car to see what there was to see. They also watched for tails. Any undercover cops would have partners around somewhere.

Once upstairs, the applicant was taken in to see Big Kahuna Lange, sitting regally on the bed. The applicant, with one undercover cop sitting behind him, would be seated in a chair facing Lange. Other cops in their gold regalia, making no effort to hide their sidearms, were sprinkled around the room.

The cop-thugs all acted like Rothmiller-Lange was Al Capone's infinitely more dangerous nephew. His cohorts did much of the talking with most of the applicants. Rothmiller acted like a man who didn't have to talk much. The room was sprinkled with bottles of Chivas Regal and other expensive booze, along with aluminum briefcases and a few carelessly thrown packets of cash.

"Just what do you think we're going to be doing?" one of Lange's men would say.

The typical response was something like "I don't know. Drugs, guns, maybe both. I don't care. I just want to get some money." Then a nervous giggle.

A few of those interviewed stated flatly they would run guns but "not anything else." But they were just a few. One pilot, an experienced gun runner, had just assumed this was a government operation. "I flew a lot of C-130s on these missions," he said. "We'll be getting government assistance, right? I'm talking about secure flight paths, landing fields, that sort of thing. From *our* government, I mean."

Lange replied, "No, I don't think the government will help us out on what we're going to be doing."

The pilot immediately backed off. "Let me think about it then," he said.

Lots of code words were used during the interviews. "Are you flying agricultural products?" which meant marijuana.

Lange or another cop would say something like, "We were flying hay [marijuana], but now we're dealing in refined products [cocaine]."

And with some of the applicants, Rothmiller hit the jackpot. They were experienced drug pilots looking to expand their contacts. They already knew other smugglers and people within the networks such as cooperative ranchers.

One of the interviewees was a wild-eyed biker from Vegas—a Brooklyn native who drove down in a chopped Honda. The pat-down turned up a dagger in his boot.

"I know you're running drugs," he said. "I want to help." He was one of the applicants who couldn't fly a plane. He wanted to be an enforcer. He dropped some names. Rothmiller knew some of those people, all of them awful sleazeballs. So Rothmiller dropped some names from the same circle of lowlifes, including some of the details he knew about them, gaining the trust of this goofball.

"I'll do anything you want," the biker said.

"What do you mean?" Rothmiller said.

"I'll whack people for you," he said.

"How can we be sure of that?" Rothmiller said.

"I'll give you the names of people I carried out hits for."

Rothmiller said he might have a problem with one of his people, someone who might be a snitch. He was going down on the next flight. "If I ask you to go down on that flight, and I tell you we don't want him coming back, is that okay?"

"No problem. Just let me know if you want it done on the strip or in the jungle."

He made one demand. He must use his best friend on any job, his best friend being an AK-47 assault rifle. "I carry an AK everywhere I go," he said. And sure enough, the parking lot detail quietly sent up word that this goofball had left an AK-47 with full banana clips wrapped inside a towel with his motorcycle. Everyone was very happy to make his acquaintance and get a full rundown on where he could be reached later.

This information was put aside along with everything else, laid out carefully, and handed over to Administrative Narcotics. A year later, Rothmiller would run into one of the narcotics detectives who was handed the case. "We're still milking that operation," he said.

As so often happened in detective work, the leads developed turned to intricate new networks of leads and ultimate arrests. One undercover narcotics man took a plane trip with one of the experienced drug pilots, who pointed out dozens of landing strips and storage areas, naming names of pilots and dealers and go-betweens and financiers, detailing flight paths and times and contacts for transactions. And that was just one source. The *Trade-A-Plane* sting in Huntington Beach turned out to be one of the most lucrative veins of intelligence ever to be tapped by the narcotics division, particularly when measured against the relatively small effort that was involved. Narcotics detectives generally had to work much harder to reap smaller rewards.

The greatest threat to the operation had come when an OCID supervisor, formerly from Internal Affairs, sought to blow the operation early in order to bust the cop applicants. "Those cops will still be there," Rothmiller pleaded. "They're not going anywhere. We can get them later. Why screw everything up now?"

Rothmiller surprised himself when he managed to ward off the pogue's destructive impulses. Meanwhile, as usual, the OCID structure and methods screamed with ironies. Time after time, the division's supervisors resisted making arrests when there should have been arrests. Then, for once, when there really was legitimate reason to show restraint, an OCID pogue wanted to move in prematurely and do what? Make arrests.

After years of stalking Sarcinelli, the time had come to make a case against him—which to an OCID detective posed a much bigger problem than it would to an ordinary policeman. Other cops could just assemble the evidence and present it to a prosecutor. But Rothmiller had to put together a case while hiding the effort from his superiors. Then he had to get some other agency to pursue the case.

Back in June 1979, Sarcinelli had been busted in a Fort Lauderdale motel room with thirteen pounds of cocaine and a $55,000 wad of cash. This appeared promising at first. But now his lawyers were tying the case up in search-and-seizure knots.

Other cops were finding Sarcinelli fingers in other pies, but no one even slapped his wrist. He remained an undeterred, active criminal who swaggered about like a skinny Goliath. It turned out that he or his intermediaries had even induced an Illinois state senator named Howard Carroll to put money into the Sarcinelli-operated real estate firm in Laguna Beach.

Rothmiller already discovered that Sarcinelli filed no income tax returns for five years, from 1975 through 1979. Wasn't anyone in IRS interested?

"But most of this stuff is based in Chicago," a Los Angeles IRS agent told Rothmiller. That was after Rothmiller finally found an IRS agent who would discuss Sarcinelli with him. This was the same agency that had been known to confiscate family tractors in lieu of back taxes. But Rothmiller was not terribly surprised by the agency's reluctance to take on Sarcinelli. He'd seen this before, particularly among federal officers. Mob guys made them skittish. Speaking off the record to Rothmiller, some of them even admitted it.

First, mob guys always had good lawyers, who might make them look dumb. So if they took a case like this one to a supervisor, he would immediately give it extra attention—the kind of attention they could do without. Plus, why go after someone who might retaliate? That was the attitude. There were lots of other cases to pursue that wouldn't disturb their sleep at night. Mobsters were vengeful people. Accidentally or on purpose, they might even hurt someone in a law enforcer's family. The people on top of federal agencies, the ones giving the orders, no doubt wanted the prosecutions. But they didn't do the work or assemble the cases.

Agents in the DEA, FBI, and IRS were civil servants with a civil servant mentality—the same mentality displayed by those OCID detectives who would rather sit outside an innocuous place like Rams headquarters to monitor the meaningless intelligence there than pursue a tough case. They got paid either way. Why bust their asses?

So although Sarcinelli resided in Los Angeles County, the IRS branch office had no interest in him. Perhaps they'd audit this guy who hadn't filed for five years, they told Rothmiller, but they didn't see a criminal prosecution in the cards. He's a Chicago guy, they said.

So next Rothmiller tried the Chicago IRS office. Here's a drug dealer and con man who doesn't pay taxes, he said. Take him.

"But he resides in Los Angeles," the Chicago agent said.

Rothmiller called up his contact on the Organized Crime Strike Force in Chicago. Did he have any chits he could call in to induce somebody to take what certainly appeared to be an open-and-shut case? A few, the Chicago detective said. He and Rothmiller made more calls, more entreaties, and finally, they moved Chicago's Rock of Gibraltar. Very reluctantly, the IRS, along with the Justice Department, undertook Sarcinelli's prosecution. The prosecutors also introduced evidence of his drug dealing. The defendant got twelve years and was sent to the federal penitentiary in Marion, Illinois, to serve his time.

Sarcinelli never knew exactly what it was that hit him. No one ever explained the chain of events that began years earlier when he opened a briefcase at Los Angeles International Airport and flashed too much cash. He had never laid eyes on Mike Rothmiller.

· 13 ·

Mexican Connections

Ageneral in the Mexican Federales lived with his family in a pleasant suburban home east of Whittier, California, during the early eighties. His name was Herman Ferriola. Ferriola was a friendly fellow with wide contacts among U.S. police and intelligence agencies. Ferriola, although he lived in California openly, appeared to be on some kind of intelligence mission. There was no doubt he had access to the deepest secrets within the Mexican intelligence community. U.S. agents, spies, and cops buzzed around him like gringo bees.

After all, the Mexican intelligence community had invaluable knowledge and contacts when it came to Latin America. The Mexican government had been run by the same political party, PRI, since the Revolution of 1913, and the overall skill of its government intelligence apparatus was one of the reasons PRI had managed to remain in power so long. Mexico was not exactly a dictatorship, nor quite a democracy. Its rulers just did what they had to do.

While PRI played a good game of calling itself a champion of a peaceful Third World Revolution against domination by the North American colossus, in fact the police and intelligence agencies it controlled kept a keen eye on subversives within Mexico. Some of the more irritating subversives had been known to just disappear and the Mexican government didn't seem to look for them afterward.

Mexico would behave like a big friendly brother to leftists in Cuba and Central America, but it also kept a close watch on them should they ever challenge PRI's dominance within Mexico. The U.S., of course, also dearly craved intelligence on these Latins of the left. At the same time, the region from the U.S. border through Central America and the Caribbean and down into the coca fields of South America boiled with big-money drug and arms deals. Agencies from a host of nations were all trying to find out what they could about the intricate plots and counterplots, deals and double-crosses that traversed the area like shifting winds.

No one seemed to know precisely what this Mexican general was doing in Los Angeles County, because Ferriola was a shrewd fellow who traded some secrets and kept others to himself. But agents and police officials tried to learn what they could from this amiable man and excellent host.

Among Ferriola's acquaintances was the police chief of North Las Vegas, Nevada. One time Ferriola's benefactor, the powerful Mexican police baron Arturo Durazo, flew up to visit Ferriola, and they took a party of friends to Las Vegas. Everyone had a rollicking good time. Afterward, when Durazo returned to Mexico, Ferriola kept a North Las Vegas police car, with insignia, sirens, lights, and all the other accoutrements parked at his California house for months. He used it from time to time, although he also had a car of his own. He said the police chief loaned it to him and there was no reason to disbelieve it. Ferriola certainly was not silly enough to steal a police car and then park it in front of his house.

But apparently Ferriola had enemies as well as friends. Once, as his daughter was driving his civilian car near their home around sunset, someone pulled up, sprayed it with bullets, and sped away. Fortunately, she wasn't hit. This was before drive-by shootings became popular. Ferriola's many police friends showed their concern, but the Americans never solved the shooting.

Among Ferriola's visitors were Mike Rothmiller and Ken Hamilton of the Organized Crime Intelligence Division of the Los Angeles Police Department. The Mexican was fast developing into one of their most valuable informants. But to gauge the value of an informant's data, it was wise to know as much as possible about the informant, and so while they befriended him, they also dug deep into his past. What they found was startling.

They traced him back to New York City, where Assistant U.S. Attorney Galvin Scott confirmed that Ferriola had originally been a major in the Colombian secret police. Years before, he had testified against some of his Colombian superiors in a drug smuggling case. He then entered the U.S. Witness Protection Program. Later, he turned up in Mexico, where he befriended Durazo. Durazo made him a colonel and ultimately a general in the Federales.

Whenever Arturo Durazo was mentioned in the U.S. press, he was always called the Mexico City police chief, true but misleading fact. Mexico City is a federal district in Mexico, something like the District of Columbia, but with a peculiar Mexican twist. As chief in the federal district, Durazo led a force of 20,000 Federales, and he was more like a combination warlord, FBI, and CIA director than police chief. He was easily the second most powerful man in Mexico, after its president, José López Portíllo, Durazo's childhood friend.

Durazo would eventually fall from grace and become a hunted man, charged with a host of crimes in Mexico, all of them relating to corruption. In fact, he would become a symbol of Mexican corruption, a man who was despised, admired, and laughed at, all at once. But when he was in power, he inspired fear. His power sprang from that fear.

Durazo lived in a Mexico City palace. On the sprawling grounds were horse stables, a garage for twenty-three cars, a bullring, dog track, gymnasium, shooting range and assorted artificial lakes. And that wasn't his only palace. When asked to explain how he amassed such wealth on a salary of approximately $5,000 a year, Durazo said he'd saved his money and made some good investments.

From 1976 until he was toppled in 1982, when someone wanted anything of consequence from the Mexican government, Durazo was the man to see.

During the last part of Durazo's rein, U.S. police and intelligence agencies had even more reason to curry his favor. They were extremely fearful that some group or combination of groups might mount a terrorist attack at the 1984 Olympics in Los Angeles.

The 1972 massacre of Israeli athletes by a Palestinian gang in Munich was a haunting memory. There were fears that various Latin, Palestinian, Iranian, perhaps even Irish Republican Army terrorists might try something awful in L.A. There was disturbing intelligence that the M-19 terrorists of Colombia and Red Brigades of Germany might be planning an Olympics scenario. Conventional wisdom said that any attackers would come through Mexico, which was less than a three-hour drive from the Games.

When Rothmiller and Hamilton explained these

concerns to Ferriola, he suggested they accompany him on a trip to Mexico City, where he would introduce them to Durazo and hatch a joint effort to thwart any terrorist plans. This seemed a bit grandiose. Durazo wasn't always an easy man to see. But Ferriola assured them he could arrange it, and although there were things about the general that didn't add up, his information always did.

The two detectives took the plan to the captain of OCID, and he agreed it would be a fine idea for the LAPD to forge this valuable link with Mexican authorities before the Olympics.

Just to make sure they weren't stepping on any brass toes, the detectives also went to see LAPD Commander Bill Rathburn in his Parker Center office. Rathburn, who is now chief of the Dallas Police Department, was in charge of Olympics security. Rathburn said everything sounded fine, but he would have to run everything by Assistant Chief Iannone. Next day, Rathburn said he had secured Iannone's approval.

Rothmiller and Hamilton also noted that if any of their superiors wished to accompany them, it could easily be arranged. There were no takers.

Everything was set, but the captain said, "What if something goes wrong?"

"What do you mean?"

"Well, the plane could crash. Anything," the captain said. "If there's any trouble, you're on your own. You will be disavowed. Understood?"

"Understood."

He proceeded to hold the paperwork on their overtime accumulation for the five-day trip. If everything went all right, they would be on department time. If not, then the department could assert the two detectives went on their own. It was a Mission Impossible, LAPD style, without the telephone booth or self-destructing briefcase.

They accepted the mission.

One more thing, said the captain. The department would not pay their airfare. It was an odd situation, all right, but the captain correctly judged his men. They were dedicated. They wouldn't scratch the journey over a matter of money. Besides, Ferriola had already told them they would be the guests of the Mexican government at the hotel. All these stipulations cast an odd shadow over the impending trip. But the lack of airfare expenses was the least surprising.

Upon arrival in Mexico City, the two detectives saw that once again Ferriola was as good as his word. They were treated like dignitaries or conquering heroes. As they registered at the Sheraton next to the U.S. Embassy, they were assisted by four armed guards. And guards stayed with them throughout their stay—one of the special flourishes, they learned later, that Durazo liked to provide to favored guests.

In Mexico, Durazo's power was like thunder, like a ferocious electric storm. It had a way of frightening its beholders at the same time it intoxicated them with its strength. When the detectives slept, the guards stood outside in the hallway with submachine guns ready, as though they were defending the Pope.

Ferriola wined them and dined them almost to the point of absurdity. Over and over he offered to send the finest whores in Mexico to their rooms. Over and over they refused. On the second day, just as he said he would, Ferriola introduced them to Durazo. Durazo was as friendly and receptive as Ferriola. He poured on charm and attention while he himself was tended to by a fawning entourage. Would they like to meet President López Portíllo for breakfast? No, please, thanks anyway, they protested. The two cops kept reminding everyone that they were just city police detectives, but the treatment continued.

Also, like good and old friends, the hosts showed complete trust. Rothmiller and Hamilton sat in police headquarters and watched while the police dispensed justice from a bazaar. At one point a group of petitioners came in to arrange the release of a family member. It was almost like planning a trip with a travel agency. Two majors handled the transaction, while Ferriola translated the proceedings for the two L.A. detectives.

The family member was charged with attempted murder. He'd stabbed a man in a fight. An older man negotiated with the officers while the wife of the accused looked on hopefully. The family wanted all charges dropped, the prisoner released.

Difficult, but not impossible, the majors advised them. After much discussion back and forth, the parties agreed on a sum—the peso equivalent of $10,000, and the negotiator immediately pulled stacks of pesos from his briefcase and began counting them out on a table.

"Where will the money go?" asked Rothmiller, always the curious cop.

The injured man would have to be compensated, Ferriola explained. The rest would go to these two majors, their colonel, the general over him, and then Durazo. Durazo took a cut of everything.

Soon after they arrived, the detectives noticed they were being followed—by Americans from the looks of it. Once again, it was difficult to tail detectives who were surveillance men themselves.

"Who are those guys?" one of the detectives asked.

"They're from your embassy," one of Durazo's men answered casually. CIA probably, Rothmiller realized.

Durazo's chief of staff, a colonel, confided to the detectives that after he first met with them, Durazo had been approached by American Embassy people he knew to be CIA. These officials told Durazo they didn't want him setting up any intelligence alliance with the LAPD.

"What did the general tell them?" Rothmiller asked.

"He said he would do what he wanted. This is his country, not theirs."

None of this sat well with Rothmiller and Hamilton. They hadn't come down here to launch any bureaucratic wars. They just wanted to keep terrorists away from Los Angeles. But after that conversation, the lavish pomp and ceremony intensified. Durazo actually made the two detectives majors in the Federales, issuing them the official badges and identification. By befriending Rothmiller and Hamilton, Durazo was asserting his own independence.

Meanwhile, the negotiations went well. Durazo was talking now about specifics, not generalities. He said his people would strengthen their border watch, monitoring all suspicious entries into Mexican territory. They would check out every blip on radar, whether by sea, air, or land. And they would share the intelligence with their U.S. friends—in the interest of a peaceful Olympics unmarred by terrorism. And all costs for these added security measures would be borne by Mexico.

But Durazo wanted something in return: access to the National Crime Information Center data on stolen vehicles. He didn't say why he craved this linkup, but it most likely had little to do with fighting crime. It was an open secret that thousands of stolen U.S. cars turned up in Mexico, and that some were driven by Mexican police, who appeared to be running some sort of used-car market featuring autos snatched north of the border. It was unclear precisely how this commerce would tie into the need for stolen vehicle data in the U.S. But in any case, Rothmiller and Hamilton tried to explain to Durazo that he was asking the wrong people for the automobile data link.

"We don't have the authority," Hamilton said. "Not even Chief Gates could do that. That's handled at the national level."

"You're in Intelligence," Durazo said. "You can do this."

"No," Rothmiller said. "The FBI, the Justice Department. But not us."

But this was all handled in friendly fashion, and Durazo never quite demanded a quid pro quo for cooperation on the Olympics. Once you were Durazo's friend, you were Durazo's friend. Meanwhile, Ferriola continued showering attention on them. He took them to see the ancient pyramids, hosted them night after night at fine restaurants. One day, near the end of their stay, two generals and two colonels came to pick up the two detectives from their hotel.

With a police escort of ten cars, they were taken to the national police academy. There they were given an official tour. A man operating a video recorder followed them around as they shook hands with everyone. They were escorted up onto a podium. And no kidding, there was a parade in their honor. They stood in review of some 2,000 cadets who passed in formation below. Once you were Durazo's friend, you were Durazo's friend.

The two detectives were not quite sure what to make of all this, but they focused on their mission. They had seen the head man, told him LAPD's concerns about the Olympics, and it appeared they were going to get exactly what the LAPD wanted.

After almost a week in Mexico City, they returned to Los Angeles on a Sunday. When they hit airport Customs, they received what felt like a bucket of cold water in the face.

"Detective Rothmiller, right?" said an agent reading a computer screen. How did he know Rothmiller was a cop?

"Right."

"Step this way, please."

Rothmiller was escorted into a nearby room, where customs agents proceeded to tear his luggage apart as though searching for priceless rubies.

"What were you doing down there?" an agent asked.

"None of your business."

His partner Hamilton was getting the same treatment in another room. The agents took all the scraps of paper they could find and photocopied them, looking for names, phone numbers, business cards, anything.

Rothmiller and Hamilton had provoked something or somebody, maybe lots of somebodies. Rothmiller had tried to put those embassy tails out of his mind, but clearly they were a fact of life that held meaning; that could not be shucked off.

The next day didn't improve. When they called in on the radio, the detectives were greeted with a Code 2. Come in and see the captain.

"What the hell were you guys doing down there?" he said accusingly.

The detectives proceeded to tell him everything that had happened in Mexico—the reception, their meetings with Durazo, the parade, everything, including the fact that L.A. Customs had treated them like anarchists trying to smuggle in plastique. The OCID captain acted like he was listening to something else, like they were detailing their exploits sacking and pillaging defenseless cities. He never said exactly what they had done wrong, but he made it clear he was displeased. He also ordered them to have nothing more to do with Olympics security.

So they went to see Rathburn. "I'm not even going to talk to you people," Rathburn said. "Talk to my lieutenant." And the commander stormed out to some meeting.

The lieutenant was some kind of robotic pogue who had no idea what was going on, so he played off spools of tape stored somewhere in his skull. "What you did was inappropriate," he said. "This whole issue is inappropriate."

A couple days later an OCID lieutenant confided to them just what had happened. "No one expected you would actually get in to see Durazo," he said. "They figured you'd wind up talking maybe to a captain or something. You're not of the appropriate rank to be meeting with Durazo."

"But we asked them to go along. We just set it up. They could have come with us."

"Yeah well, I don't know about that," the lieutenant said. "But they're all pissed. Iannone, Rathburn, Vernon, everybody. When they found out what you were doing down there, they hit the roof."

The brass hats had been trying to set up connections with Durazo for months, the lieutenant said, and it had been like trying to untangle a mess of coat hangers. They got nowhere. They expected Rothmiller and Hamilton to meet the same fate. For these two lowly detectives to succeed where they had failed was more than they could bear. The detectives should do their best to try to help everyone forget the whole embarrassing episode.

And it turned out that the superpogues were about as angry with Rothmiller as he'd ever seen them. His superiors had been upset with him before, of course, usually because he pursued a case or a criminal they didn't want pursued. But this time he thought he might actually get bounced from the division. They acted like he and Hamilton were OCID's very own Manson Family. He had strayed into protocol territory and there was nothing so riled as a pogue whose protocol had been preempted.

While the two detectives were trying to lie low, Ferriola returned from Mexico and asked about getting started on some of the linkups Durazo had agreed to.

"It looks like we'll have to forget all that," Rothmiller explained.

At least the paperwork went through so that Rothmiller and Hamilton were not on their own time for the Mission Impossible. The department admitted they had been gone on an LAPD assignment after all, even though they had blundered by accomplishing the mission.

Those tails back in Mexico City stayed on Rothmiller's mind. He asked a CIA contact, an oil firm executive, what he thought about establishing an antiterrorist plan with Durazo.

"I'll get back to you," the spook said.

And he did. "[CIA Director William] Casey thinks it's a good idea," the man said. "But not at this time. He says the time isn't right."

What could that mean? The Olympics would take place in 1984. When was the best time to plan for them? 1985? But that was the message, and Rothmiller could get no more out of him.

A pattern was developing. The problems of policing Los Angeles were becoming tangled in international developments. So informants like Ferriola were becoming more crucial to the work of policemen. Rothmiller worked like a cop, not an agent. But cops, if they were good cops, found things out. In this new arena particularly, knowledge could be a dangerous commodity.

Along about this time Ferriola began to tell them about a man they knew nothing about. You should watch this man, he said. He's a man Los Angeles police should know about. The man's name was Robert Terry.

Rothmiller started checking out Terry. He found a story that would fit well in a preposterous film. An ex–New York City policeman, Terry had pleaded guilty in 1966 to working as a courier for a counterfeit currency ring. He testified against his accomplices and received a suspended sentence. He then entered the U.S. Witness Protection Program and disappeared. When Rothmiller started looking into him, Terry had already reemerged in Southern California, leading an entirely new existence.

This Robert Terry lived in a fabulous penthouse in pricy Marina Del Rey. He owned aircraft leasing and charter services that did a lot of business out of Florida into Latin America. There was a complex interlocking of firms. Among them were entities called Airspur, Aero Industries, Inc., and Consolidated Aircraft. He threw lavish parties and didn't mind the spotlight. He donated $25,000 toward a new set of White House china, and afterward posed for a photo with a grateful Nancy Reagan, who said she would pass the check on to charity. He was also an important booster of Mayor Bradley, who was gearing up for the 1982 California gubernatorial election.

This new life wouldn't have appeared suspicious were he not a convicted smuggler operating air charter services. That, and the fact that he hired bodyguards who never left his side.

And he was trying to sell machine guns to Mexico. Ferriola said Terry claimed to have big connections in Washington. His fleet of planes was ferrying guns to Central America, Ferriola said, with the blessings of Washington. But most disturbing, Ferriola said, these appeared to be round-trip transactions. Ferriola's information was that the planes—big, modern C-130s—were transporting drugs on the return trip north.

As Rothmiller did some checking of his own, he learned Terry also had a history of ties to big-time mobsters. Among them was Charlie ("Chuck the Knife") Delmonico, a convicted extortionist from Miami, who was linked to both Chicago and New Jersey Mafia families.

Ferriola stayed close to Terry and milked him for more information. Terry kept trying to push this machine gun transaction. He was offering Ferriola a commission if he would be the middleman and fly to Mexico City with him on one of Terry's private jets. He wanted to sell the guns to Durazo. Ferriola met Terry in Las Vegas and Terry gave him two machine gun samples. Take these to Mexico, he said, and have them tried out. We should do business.

Terry goes to Washington a lot, Ferriola said. He has big connections, including the CIA. He claims to be tight with Attorney General Edwin Meese. He's flying these guns to the Contras.

Rothmiller had never before heard the word *contra.* It was a word not yet recognized by Americans. They're rightwing rebels fighting the Nicaraguan Sandinistas, Ferriola explained.

Rothmiller figured if Ferriola was just 70 percent accurate, there was something terribly nasty going on here. And Herman Ferriola was almost always more than 70 percent accurate. In the intelligence world, he was a Ted Williams–type hitter.

"See if you can find out the next time this guy's going to Washington," Rothmiller told Ferriola. "Let's see just what he does there."

Meanwhile, Rothmiller shared his material on Terry with an IRS intelligence agent he'd worked with before. This Terry could be breaking an assortment of federal laws—the Neutrality Act, narcotics statutes, income tax avoidance, and who knows what else? The agent arranged to set up a Washington tail on Terry.

Rothmiller was moving in an arena that seemed a galaxy removed from the time and place some ten years earlier, when he'd been a rookie patrolling the Wilshire district. Yet it was the same world. He was just being a cop trying to stop bad guys.

Ferriola called Rothmiller with the information. He had a tip on a forthcoming Terry trip to Washington.

The IRS watched Terry step off the airliner. He was met by a man whose manner and attire suggested he was a government official. They entered a government car and headed toward CIA headquarters at Langley, Virginia. Then the IRS surveillance team lost the car.

The next day the agents picked up Terry's tail again. He went into the Executive Office Building of the White House. IRS intelligence made inquiries at the White House. The White House stonewalled. IRS investigators decided to pour on the heat. They kicked the case up the line to their top people. They were stonewalled, too. They couldn't find out just what business Terry was transacting or the identity of the officials who were talking to him.

Along about this time something happened back in California that seemed almost designed to stop the flow of information from the West Coast end of the case. Immigration and Naturalization Service agents suddenly snatched Ferriola. They were in such a hurry to get him out of the country, they evidently forgot Ferriola's family also lacked the necessary residence papers. His family was left behind.

Frantic, Mrs. Ferriola called Rothmiller. He shot down to the Federal Building in downtown L.A. and found someone on the federal Organized

Crime Strike Force to intercede. It turned out that Ferriola was moments away from being spirited down to the INS holding station at El Centro, in the desert east of San Diego. The expulsion was being worked at the speed of light. But the call came in time. A hold was placed on the peculiar deportation of this Mexican general.

Now Ferriola was frantic as well. His business required him to make periodic trips between California and Mexico, but there was a court date hanging over his head, and under the terms of his release, he could not leave the country. Eventually he calmed down, and Ferriola called a border patrol commander, making special arrangements with him to make his crossings without any interruptions from some distant court process.

But Ferriola's information on Terry had dried up. Terry now gave him the cold shoulder. He'd been warned. Perhaps he found out Ferriola was related to the inquiries and surveillance. Or perhaps he just decided to stop talking to whomever he'd been talking to. It didn't require any great detective work. A phone tap or two, a bug here and there would do it.

New bodyguards patrolled outside Terry's penthouse. They were off-duty LAPD officers. And everything on Terry was locked up tight, as though he'd entered a cocoon.

Rothmiller began to wonder if the Terry business could be somehow related to the CIA's stance against increased surveillance on Mexico's southern border with Guatemala. This is not the right time, the CIA contact had said.

· 14 ·

Shots in the Night

The Organized Crime Strike Force in L.A. was investigating a wealthy businessman living in east Los Angeles County who, like Robert Terry, was reputedly involved in smuggling guns south and drugs north across America's southern borders. An OCID lieutenant who sat on the strike force called Rothmiller and Hamilton onto the case.

This suspect was making discreet inquiries, trying to find more aircraft suitable for the special circumstances that prevailed in these journeys. By now Rothmiller was quite familiar with what smugglers needed—good cargo planes that didn't need a lot of coddling. There never seemed to be enough of such planes. Often they had to be ditched after one run and a quick unloading.

Rothmiller checked with Ferriola. Ferriola said he had heard nothing about this businessman, but if Rothmiller needed his help to snare him, Ferriola would be glad to provide it. That's when Rothmiller hatched a plan to see if they could bring this guy out in the open.

Rothmiller would approach intermediaries and tell them that he could provide access to as many as two thousand cargo aircraft that had been seized for smuggling by Mexico and were now mothballed south of the border. Many of the planes were in excellent repair and stored in the Tijuana area.

For a commission, Rothmiller could arrange an ongoing relationship supplying impounded aircraft right back into the smuggling trade. Mexico, he would say, might even be willing to sell them for pennies on the dollar to a quiet, dependable purchaser. This would be similar, really, to what the U.S. did at its public auctions of seized boats, planes, and vehicles. The difference was that money received at U.S. auctions had a much better chance of going into the proper government coffers than would the sums received by Mexican officials.

Rothmiller figured that if he could get inside this smuggling network posing as a crooked cop with connections in Mexico, then for once authorities might be able to indict top people instead of the small fish netted infrequently along the border. He took the plan to his superiors, of course. Otherwise he could have been setting himself up for possible arrest as a rogue cop.

Rothmiller received a go signal from his lieutenant. Meanwhile, the lieutenant quietly relayed information on the plan to the Organized Crime Strike Force.

Almost coincidentally, investigators were getting indications that this same tycoon was also part of the coalition attempting to legalize gambling at Lake Havasu, Arizona. It wasn't entirely a coincidence. Hustlers involved in these high-level criminal schemes tended to coalesce like merchants at a fair. One scam was never enough. They were the same as the petty crooks Rothmiller observed in bars and greasy spoons; they just played for higher stakes.

One of the informants implicating the L.A.

County businessman was Joe Agosto, a Kansas City mobster who'd moved to San Clemente. Agosto was yet another relocated federal witness living a fairly comfortable life outside prison providing information on the doings of his acquaintances.

Rothmiller was never terribly comfortable sharing information that could be physically dangerous to himself or the detectives he worked with. He was even less comfortable turning it over to the federal strike force. These Organized Crime Strike Forces located in the nation's major cities pulled investigators from all major federal investigation teams in their geographical areas—DEA; FBI; Customs; Treasury; Alcohol, Tobacco, and Firearms. The theory was that each member of the team would contribute different expertise and that the sum of the whole would then be greater than its parts.

But what looked like a great idea on paper didn't work out as well in the flesh. Supervisors from the feeding agencies often used the same tactics as professional sports teams when they had to expose players to an expansion draft. They would clean out the bottom of their rosters by sending over their duds and leftovers.

But Rothmiller went forward. He finagled an introduction to a weapons dealer and ex-cop who had business connections with the East L.A. businessman. The weapons dealer said that he and the businessman's adult son sometimes went target shooting in the hills with machine guns.

Rothmiller, hinting at what he could offer a smuggling ring, asked the businessman to arrange for a meeting. The arms dealer promised to set up an introduction to the son, who, he said, handled that end of the business.

Already this case was connected to other cases, like a network of waterways all flowing in the same direction. Now there was yet another confluence. Rothmiller, looking through the federal strike force files, saw a picture of one of its informants and stopped. His name was Jack Ingraham. "I've seen this guy," Rothmiller said. "Where does he live?"

It turned out that Ingraham, a Canadian convicted of smuggling who was connected to the Chicago mob, had turned his coat and entered the federal Witness Protection Program. The feds had relocated Ingraham to a house about 100 yards from Rothmiller's residence. Rothmiller had seen him many times around the neighborhood.

The federal government seemed to be pouring relocated witnesses into Orange County with distressing regularity. When they made their snitch deals, the snitches often demanded relocation to a warm climate, and for some reason known only to the federal government, Orange County frequently topped its list as a warm destination.

Ingraham worked at an aircraft leasing office at John Wayne Airport in Orange County. He had a commercial relationship with the same East L.A. County businessman who was under suspicion.

When Rothmiller was able to pinpoint just what information Ingraham was providing, he was also able to confirm, through his own information network, that Ingraham was feeding a good deal of false data into the system. Rothmiller tried to warn strike force agents, but they continued to rely on Ingraham. Ingraham and the customs agent who supposedly controlled him were having barbecues together. It was one of those symbiotic relationships between cop and criminal that appeared to be working much better for the parasite than the host.

Weeks went by. Rothmiller waited for his go-between to get back to him on the meeting with the businessman's son. Then one day Rothmiller spotted something across the street from his house that he didn't like at all—Ingraham in a black Mercedes. After he sat there awhile, Ingraham backed up a bit to peer along the side of the house.

Then he pulled forward to look over the other side. He was casing the place like a burglar. Rothmiller notified the strike force.

Also about this time Rothmiller received a threatening phone call: "Keep your nose out of our business or you're dead."

Meanwhile, he continued working other cases. He hoped that the still-extant pogue animosity stemming from the Mexico City trip would gradually blow over.

Rothmiller and his partner were also taking a private crash course from a banker acquaintance so they could set up yet another sting. Their plan was to offer no-questions-asked offshore banking out of Western Samoa or Guam and see who showed up. They theorized that the Cayman Islands connections were drawing too much heat, and so international criminals would be eager to find new offshore money laundries.

Along about this time Rothmiller developed an informant who was a reserve deputy sheriff in Kern County, north of Los Angeles. The deputy believed he had found evidence pointing to corruption within the sheriff's department there. He said there were even payoffs being taken from drug smugglers. He didn't trust the District Attorney's Office in Kern County, but he was willing to talk to Rothmiller, who set up a meeting.

The day of the meeting Rothmiller was on a surveillance at John Wayne Airport with his lieutenant and other detectives. They wanted to see what Ingraham was up to. Rothmiller told his lieutenant about the appointment in Kern County and left the surveillance in the early afternoon. He gassed up at Parker Center and drove to Mojave, about 90 miles out in the desert. He and his informant spoke for several hours. About 10 P.M., Rothmiller left for home.

"That night a friend called Mike," Nancy

Rothmiller recalls, "and I told him he was meeting someone in Mojave. 'Mojave?' he said. 'I know the place. It's full of rednecks. Not a good place for a cop to be alone at night.'

"You know Mike was always meeting informants in strange places at strange times and I never lay up nights worrying about him. That night I remember I woke up. I heard a motorcycle outside. I thought it was a car at first. I dozed off. Then the doorbell was ringing. It was a police officer."

Rothmiller got home just before midnight, dead tired after a long night of talking and then driving. When he pulled into his driveway, he remembered. He had to drop off a note in the mailbox of a neighbor, who was also a cop. Several couples were planning a trip to Maui together and he had to leave his friend some information about the arrangements.

Rothmiller pulled back out of the driveway and headed toward the house, only a few blocks away. He was dimly aware of a motorcycle behind him, perhaps three hundred yards back. There was nothing else stirring at that hour. He entered a serpentine road that led into another housing tract and the motorcycle drew closer.

Somebody's screwing around with me, he thought. He punched the gas pedal. The biker stayed with him, then looked like he was going to pass. Rothmiller pulled in the center of the street. Then he heard the popping of a weapon and swerved off the road.

"The police officer told me Mike had been in an accident and that I should go to the hospital," Nancy remembers. "I said, 'What kind of accident?' He said, 'A car accident.' I told him, 'My husband's an excellent driver. It wasn't really a car accident, was it?' He wouldn't look me in the eye."

The Huntington Beach cop didn't offer to take

her to the hospital, so she asked for directions and drove over alone.

When she arrived, a staff member said Mike was in surgery, and that doctors were removing a bullet from his body. "Your mind is not ready to absorb all that," she explains. "So I was thinking that perhaps it wasn't real."

After about twenty minutes, someone told her surgeons removed a glass fragment. It wasn't a bullet after all. Then she got to see him, but others were grilling him relentlessly. Over and over, the same questions were repeated. She began to faint, and a nurse helped her. Then the cops told her she couldn't go home, that her home was now unsafe.

· 15 ·

Rejection, Redemption

Ingraham flunked a polygraph on the shooting," the OCID lieutenant confided to Rothmiller. "He was planning to split the country. Somebody paid him a lot of money."

Then there was a tie-in. Ingraham was a federally protected witness. And he was protected because he was afraid of someone. So there had to be a way to lean on him and get the truth.

Rothmiller, sitting back at home, trying to find a less painful way to position his body, tried to absorb this new information. He was surrounded by SWAT teamers, a blaring TV, ringing phones, the unrelenting pain.

His lieutenant would come by once in a while and give him an update, advise him yet again to be careful what he said to Huntington Beach police. Meanwhile, the doctors had given it to him straight. This kind of back trauma was unpredictable. It could cause many problems beyond the pain and immobility he now felt. It could trigger impotence, for instance. It could even attack his bowels.

Possibly the pain might never cease. Meanwhile, he was still angry and shaken, awash in hurt. And suddenly feeling very helpless. He kept an M-1 carbine by his side. The circumstances were so bizarre it didn't really seem out of place. Not with SWAT team people and their weapons all over the place.

He took some comfort in the fact that it appeared OCID detectives were moving fast to solve the shooting. Ingraham was a practiced liar, but he'd informed before. He could be made to inform again. They'd trip him up. If anyone knew how, they did.

While Mike was in the hospital, Nancy had stayed with her parents. The police told her it was still too dangerous to go back to work. When Mike was released, she returned home. But life was crazy there, it wasn't her home anymore. It was occupied territory. When she went out to the garage to put laundry in the washing machine, she was accompanied by a woman SWAT officer carrying a weapon. Anyone wishing to enter her house was closely questioned by cops wearing blank stares.

"I'm going back to work," she stated. She missed the bank.

A SWAT bodyguard would have to stay with her, the department replied.

"I'm not going to work with a guard watching me. I can't be guarded all my life anyway," she said.

Finally they gave in, warning her she was making a mistake.

"Are you checking any other leads?" Rothmiller asked the lieutenant. "Any of the other cases?"

"No, we're not even looking. We know who's behind this," the lieutenant said. "But don't tell Huntington Beach much. Make them think you're cooperating, but don't tell them anything. We want to take it, understand?"

If Huntington Beach PD had been compromised, as the lieutenant told him, that clearly left Rothmiller only one alternative. He would have to trust OCID.

But he couldn't forget something else the lieutenant told him the night of the shooting when Rothmiller had been lying on the gurney. It was after the lieutenant had notified the OCID captain about the shooting.

The captain's first words weren't "How is he?" said the lieutenant, relaying the conversation to Rothmiller. They were "What was he doing out there with a city car?"

Test Rothmiller's blood for alcohol and find out if he had any girlfriends, the captain ordered. This sounded to him like the work of a jealous husband.

No, no, you don't know Mike, Rothmiller's lieutenant reportedly replied to the captain.

This particular captain was a former Internal Affairs Division person. Although now Rothmiller desperately needed OCID to solve this case, he also knew the unit worked in strange, sometimes inexplicable ways and he couldn't be sure how the pogues might react.

Rothmiller realized this shooting could attract the one thing OCID would not stand for—media attention. The story had been successfully hushed up so far, but too many people knew about it— Huntington Beach police, for instance. If Huntington Beach made arrests, how could that be kept out of the papers? And no one knew better than Rothmiller how much OCID hated arrests.

When the lieutenant promised Rothmiller that the unit would handle this, Rothmiller kept telling himself that it would do just that—handle it, whatever it took. Rothmiller waited at home for something to break. It wasn't an easy place to wait.

"We had a circus at our house," Nancy recalls.

"We had to warn anyone who was coming over about the SWAT team. It just became an impossible situation."

A friend with a vacant beach house offered it to the Rothmillers. The LAPD let them stay there SWAT-less and they did for two weeks. But Mike remained jittery, in pain, unable to sleep. It didn't seem like the physical therapy was working. His right leg was numb all the time, as though perennially asleep.

An OCID detective who lived nearby quizzed Rothmiller on what the doctors were saying about his condition. They didn't know. The disability could be permanent. Or it might be remedied with surgery.

You've got to file a Workers' Compensation claim, the detective told him. This was a pro forma act to establish that his injury was work-related. He had only one year from the date of injury to file.

You better see an attorney and protect yourself, the detective told him. Rothmiller didn't want to even talk about this with the SWAT team there. Other friends were offering similar advice.

Finally a friend persuaded him to see an attorney, driving him to a lawyer's office in the San Fernando Valley. "Let me talk to your medical liaison officer," the lawyer told Rothmiller. "This shouldn't be any trouble."

"The guy I work for is a pretty weird egg," Rothmiller objected. "This could be a lot of trouble."

"I just want to talk to them," the lawyer said. "It's perfectly normal. They'll expect it." Rothmiller relented.

The next day the lawyer called Rothmiller and told him he'd talked to the department's medical liaison. "He advises you to file a claim so your back injury will be medically covered. You could get better and forget about it, and then run into physical problems years later. This way you'd still be covered. It's what he advises."

A finding in his favor would not set Rothmiller up on some kind of lifetime dole, but it could pay him a small stipend for a year or so, depending on the extent of injury.

"Let me think about it awhile," he told his lawyer.

What he truly wanted was to remain an OCID detective. But if he filed any kind of claim, no matter how just, he feared it might jeopardize his position in his mysterious unit. However, if he didn't file to protect his rights and was unable to return to work because of his injuries, he would be left with nothing. He thought about it a couple days, talked it over with Nancy, and finally called his attorney, telling him to proceed with the claim.

Shortly afterward Rothmiller's attorney reported talking to the cops' medical liaison. "He says your captain went ballistic. He was screaming at him over the phone. 'What's that motherfucker trying to pull? He won't get away with this!' "

A month went by and there was no news on the shooting. Rothmiller feared OCID was shining him on. He was no longer quite so prepared to believe the lieutenant's story that a Huntington Beach investigator had been paid off.

Then a friend offered Mike and Nancy the opportunity to stay at his cabin at Mammoth Lakes in Northern California. It would be vacant for a week. Nancy couldn't get away now, but Mike could go up there and fish, get away from this. Go ahead, his doctors said.

Rothmiller's captain had a subordinate call him with the bad news. To travel, he would have to drop his Injured on Duty status, then try to alter it back again upon his return. This would require making the rounds of all his doctors twice: to drop, then restore his status. Rothmiller was sure the doctors wouldn't sign in the first place, they would maintain his Injured status was correct.

This seemed suddenly like a hostile game, some piece of obstinacy to harass him. He was being treated as the enemy, like someone who'd committed contempt of cop.

Rothmiller called his captain for an explanation. Why couldn't he go fishing? It seemed such a simple request. The department could guard Nancy. SWAT had recently been taken off the case and OCID detectives were now guarding the house. This gave the captain even more power over the Rothmillers' life. His men were inside every minute.

"If you really cared for your wife," the captain told him, "you'd stay home and guard her yourself."

The LAPD is a paramilitary organization. Its detectives do not quarrel with captains. Instead, Rothmiller slammed the phone down. He called back the next moment. "You motherfucker!" he screamed. "If you even try to fuck with me anymore, I'm going to the press. I'll tell them everything! I'll bury you motherfuckers!"

He didn't go fishing at Mammoth Lakes.

He was nearing the end of his rope. Normally a neat man, he now shaved intermittently. He sat around the house, waiting for his physical therapy and medical appointments.

The Rothmillers had already paid for their Hawaii trip before the shooting, and they both looked forward to escaping the madness of their homelife. All of Rothmiller's doctors encouraged him to take the trip. It was more like an order than a suggestion.

Five days before the scheduled Hawaii departure, the OCID captain tried to use a club studded with regulations and paperwork to prevent this trip too. He demanded new rounds of signatures from the doctors. Again, he insisted they would have to remove Rothmiller from Injured status. The trip was now a Holy Grail to the Rothmillers. Perhaps it would turn everything around, undo all the terrible realities that had entered their life during those split seconds on a dark street.

"That's it!" Rothmiller again threatened the obstinate captain. "I'm dropping the hammer! I'm going to the press about everything!" He didn't specify what he meant, but there was no longer any pretense of respect between the two men.

Hours later a detective called with a message from the captain. He had dropped his objections to the trip as long as Rothmiller obtained the orthopedic surgeon's approval. The doctor had already said he could swim, snorkel, anything. If pain increased, Rothmiller would have to ease off. That was the way he'd have to live from then on, and Hawaii was a good place to start.

A few days before their departure, the lieutenant stopped by and told Rothmiller to stop talking to Huntington Beach altogether. "We're taking this thing over," the lieutenant said.

"Why?"

"They're not handling it right."

If Rothmiller disobeyed and spoke to Huntington Beach now, it would be insubordination, which could get him fired. If he obeyed, Huntington Beach would no doubt believe he was covering something up. He obeyed.

Just before he left for Maui, an OCID detective came over and gave Rothmiller an envelope. "Do me a favor, Mike. Keep this for a while." Inside were some OCID intelligence reports that had no relationship to Rothmiller's cases. He took the envelope. When the detective left, Rothmiller dropped it at a friend's house for safekeeping.

In Hawaii, Rothmiller went down to the pool the first day and recognized someone from the LAPD. He was sure of it!

He knew this trick. When detectives wanted to annoy someone, they would pop out of the bushes. We're watching you, was the message, and you don't know when we'll be back. We might return at any time.

Now everywhere Rothmiller went around the hotel, this guy turned up like a puppy, though he was actually trying not to be noticed. When Rothmiller looked in his direction, the man would look away or walk off, only to turn up again shortly afterwards. He was one of the worst detectives on foot surveillance Rothmiller had ever seen. It was like being followed by a school kid. But Rothmiller was still a real detective; he found out the cop's name. When he returned home ten days later, he learned the cop worked in Internal Affairs. The department had sent someone all the way to Maui to try to get something on Rothmiller.

When the Rothmillers returned, it was to an unguarded house, a mixed blessing.

When confronted, at first the lieutenant denied Rothmiller had been followed to Hawaii. "You're imagining things, Mike," he said soothingly. "You're under stress. You must be hallucinating."

"You motherfucker!" Rothmiller screamed at his lieutenant. "I'm going to kick the shit out of you!"

In a less frenzied moment, Rothmiller was able to get independent confirmation that he had been followed. He called the lieutenant back. This time the lieutenant, faced with the evidence, admitted the surveillance. "But don't talk to anybody about this," he said.

"Fuck you. I'll talk to anybody I want."

A few days later, Rothmiller started getting phantom phone calls. He would answer. No one was there. This continued, day in and day out. Sometimes the phone rang every fifteen minutes for hours on end. The calls came always when Nancy was gone, stopping when she came home. He put a recorder on his phone, hoping to trip up his tormentors.

"They were pushing, pushing, pushing," Nancy remembers, "and we didn't know why. They were trying to push him over the edge."

Returning home one day, Rothmiller found it had been ransacked. Someone had looked through his papers. He believed they were looking for the envelope containing intelligence reports that had been given to him earlier. Taking home official intelligence files was a felony. OCID also confiscated his guns.

One of Rothmiller's pistols was a .22-caliber. He had been shot at with a .22. When OCID removed his weapons, it sent his .22-caliber pistol over to ballistics to see if Rothmiller's shooting had been faked. But there was no match with the slugs embedded in his car, so the department denied running the test. Rothmiller's lawyer ran down the file and obtained a copy.

This told Rothmiller two things. The department would now claim no one had shot at him that night. And someone in OCID actually believed, or at least hoped, there had been no shooting. Otherwise there would have been no ballistics test. If there was no shooting, there was no need for arrest, no need for publicity.

After this, the department pursued and harassed Rothmiller as though he were a politician who was loathed but not feared. There was no need for subtlety or to cover tracks. Some of the things the department did over the next several months seemed surreal.

For starters, OCID warned LAPD friends of the Rothmillers to stay away from them. It was clearly an effort to isolate them to remove their support network. It led to much pain. On the other hand, some cop families stood up and said this was an illegal order they would not obey. In this way the Rothmillers learned who their true friends were.

The Workers' Compensation case became a sacred principle. If the pogues would ruin his career because he filed the claim, then at least he would do all he could to win it. The doctors said he had suffered nerve damage in the accident, and that it could not be repaired. Surgery would be useless.

Rothmiller hired an attorney, Mary Ann Healy, formerly a nun for twenty-five years. She provided precisely the correct portions of legal expertise and human understanding. She would regularly drive down at night after work and raise Rothmiller's spirits.

When Rothmiller gave a deposition in relation to his claim, a lawyer for the city inexplicably led the questioning into the realm of political espionage. It was an odd moment for Rothmiller. He had always kept the secrets, even after he had threatened to reveal them. Now, under oath, he was being asked specifically about what he and others did in OCID. He told the truth.

The city's lawyer realized his error and cut off the line of questioning. But the ACLU, at the time filing suit to get at the Public Disorder Intelligence Division files, learned of the deposition and promptly subpoenaed Rothmiller. The city tried to prevent his testimony, but their motion to do so failed. At last the news media discovered OCID and began to report on these depositions.

The department suspended Rothmiller without pay and filed seventeen misconduct charges. Then, contrary to its own rules, the LAPD leaked the charges against him to the press in order to discredit the veteran cop. Rothmiller was a disgruntled cop who'd faked his own shooting, said the department. And it ordered Rothmiller not to talk to reporters. His attorney advised him to obey the order and he did. Day after day he was lashed in print. Only once did a reporter find him and ask for his side. "No comment," he said.

One day someone called Nancy's employer and reported Mike had been killed in a car accident.

An Internal Affairs Division detective would periodically drive by the house and honk his horn.

One day Rothmiller and a friend, a retired federal agent, surveilled the IAD man after he swung by. They followed him to the freeway, then pulled alongside. He turned, saw Rothmiller, and cut across three lanes to an exit, nearly triggering a pileup.

Someone burgled Rothmiller's locker at OCID—right inside a police station! He lost personal effects and his uniforms.

One day Nancy and Mike stepped out of an elevator in his doctor's building and two Internal Affairs investigators were standing there waiting. Popping out of bushes again. This time Nancy did the screaming. Nancy is 5 feet, 2 inches, 105 pounds. The cops backed off.

Jack Ingraham, who had failed the polygraph regarding his answers to questions about his knowledge of Rothmiller and the shooting, was swept away into another bureaucratic corner of the federal Witness Protection Program, given a new identity, a new location. Now Rothmiller couldn't subpoena him.

In June 1983, while Mike was up at Mammoth Lakes and Nancy was at work, the Huntington Beach Police Department said it received a call from the Rothmiller residence. The caller mumbled a suicide threat and hung up.

A Huntington Beach cop arrived at the Rothmiller home. It just so happened that an ex-LAPD cop who lived nearby went over to see what was going on. He watched the Huntington

Beach policeman meet two plainclothes LAPD detectives who soon pulled up in an LAPD unmarked car. The detectives went around the back of the house and broke a window. They knew the location of the secret switch to the alarm system and shut it off immediately. The only person besides Rothmiller who knew the location of the switch was an OCID detective who'd helped Rothmiller install the system.

The ex-cop observing the two detectives saw them disappear into Rothmiller's house. They didn't reappear for a half hour or so. Later the Rothmillers discovered someone had rifled through their legal papers and documents, particularly tax records. When Rothmiller's attorney asked for the tape of the 911 emergency call supposedly made from the Rothmiller residence, the police said it could not be found.

Years later one of the black-bag detectives who'd responded to the stiffed call would admit it to another detective in the unit, "You know we can't talk about that stuff," shutting off the discussion. Subsequent to the break-in, the IRS audited the Rothmillers' 1983 returns.

Rothmiller was gaining a little leverage. Once the case entered the legal system, the dirty tricks held less power, particularly when they were used against someone who knew the tricks.

In response to questions for a deposition, Rothmiller named the East L.A. County businessman connected to Ingraham who was suspected of being a smuggler. The businessman sued Rothmiller, as did the weapons dealer who was supposed to get Rothmiller in touch with the businessman's son. Both cases were later dropped.

Finally, on February 28, 1984, eighteen months after the shooting, the judge ruled in favor of Rothmiller in his Workers' Compensation claim. The judge further declared that the shooting had in fact occurred and that Rothmiller was clearly seriously injured in the attack. Rothmiller, the judge found, "was investigated and harassed" because he filed the claim.

The judge concluded that as part of its harassment campaign, the LAPD tracked Rothmiller all the way to Hawaii to keep him under surveillance. The LAPD did not deny this and refused to state why it was done, the judge noted.

The judge accused the LAPD of suppressing evidence when it learned that Ingraham had failed a lie detector exam about the shooting. Also, Rothmiller's attorney had produced three neighbors who heard a motorcycle racing its engine as well as sound that might have been gunfire.

Furthermore, the judge found that the car had been shot at and that, contrary to the LAPD's allegations, Rothmiller had every right to be driving it. He noted that the LAPD and Huntington Beach department had ballistics experts, yet they would not explain why the experts were not called to testify. The presumption was that their testimony would have aided Rothmiller's case. Instead, other detectives who were not ballistics experts testified.

The judge addressed all seventeen charges and answered all of them in Rothmiller's favor. The department had even claimed Rothmiller left for Mojave without authorization and that he "improperly utilized a City-owned vehicle to conduct personal business." The judge ordered the department to reinstate Rothmiller.

The department offered him a living-death desk job in juvenile narcotics. Instead, he resigned. He had his victory. He collected about $25,000 in the case, which just about paid his legal fees.

By the time Rothmiller won his ruling the news media were no longer interested. The story was cold. Few of the people who read the department's accusations against him ever read of the ultimate disposition of the case.

He applied for a partial pension based on his stress and injuries, but the retirement board ruled he was now well enough to function without it. Denied.

The LAPD was changing the guard when Rothmiller cowrote this book. He hoped the new administration might see this as a golden opportunity to curtail the abuses of its secret police. It might even see to it that in the future, the Organized Crime Intelligence Division focused on mobsters and the Anti-Terrorist Division pursued terrorists.

But he knew that it was impossible to underestimate the torrential power of preestablished behavior on the LAPD. So the department could well react as always and just attack the whistle-blowers.

Or it might be clever this time: admit past mistakes, promise to behave, and then do business in the same old way.

Even while fighting for his own life and name, Rothmiller never really penetrated the unfathomable bureaucratic priorities of the pogues. He could make educated guesses why the department drummed him out of OCID rather than pursue the case against his attacker, but he could never be sure what the motivating factors were. Rothmiller would never be sure who tried to kill him or why. It was a perfect irony that once again OCID had used its influence to hinder a criminal arrest. During the five years Rothmiller spent within the Organized Crime Intelligence Division, it never arrested one mobster.

Not one.

Postscript

J oe Agosto and Tony Acardo died of natural
causes.

Tony "the Ant" Spilotro and his brother
Michael Spilotro were found beaten to death and
dumped in an Indiana cornfield on the outskirts of
Chicago in June 1986.

Sam Sarcinelli, after being sentenced to twelve
years on income tax charges related to his drug
trade, pleaded guilty in April 1987, while a federal
prisoner at Marion, Illinois, to a stock manipula-
tion scheme. As a government witness, he testified
against four brokers who received four to six years
apiece. He was subsequently released and is now
selling restaurant supplies in Southern California.

Phillip De Petro, alias Sleazy, alias Mickey
Rooney, was not murdered and buried in the
desert, despite rumors to the contrary. The story
was a cover arranged for him by the LAPD so the
super-informant could quietly disappear from the
L.A. crime scene. He eventually broke cover and is
now employed at a trucking firm in Southern
California.

Max Mayberry, his shooting partner, is still in
state prison.

Willy Cunningham, the pimp who complained
that a deputy chief was demanding free sex from
one of his hookers, died in a mysterious shooting.

Assistant Chief Marvin Iannone left the LAPD
to become Beverly Hills Police Chief.

Detective Ken Hamilton of OCID was with the family of the toppled police baron Arturo Durazo, in June 1984 in Puerto Rico when federal authorities arrested Durazo. Durazo had fled Mexico after being charged with corruption. Hamilton, who contended Durazo was preparing to surrender, was transferred out of OCID. He is now a burglary detective.

Detective Frank Skrah of OCID is planning to retire soon and coach community college baseball in Northern California.

Pete Acuna, Rothmiller's former vice partner, graduated from law school, quit the LAPD, and is a criminal attorney in Los Angeles.

The OCID detectives who were bugging their captain's office for years found out that he had one-upped them. All the while, he had been spying on them with a bug and video camera concealed inside a phony ceiling sprinkler.

The vice sergeant who said he manufactured a lewd conduct case against an innocent man has since been promoted. He holds a very senior position in the LAPD.

The Los Angeles voters in June 1992 passed Charter Amendment F by a more than 2–1 margin. It gives City Hall the power to remove the LAPD chief, limits the chief's tenure to two five-year terms, and provides more civilian review of officer misconduct.

Mike Rothmiller is an independent TV producer who specializes in sports and outdoor shows, and he is now an author as well.

Quiet teams are still operating out of Fort Davis.

An *Original* Publication of POCKET BOOKS

POCKET BOOKS, a division of Simon & Schuster Inc.
1230 Avenue of the Americas, New York, NY 10020

ISBN: 0-671-79657-7

First Pocket Books printing August 1992

10 9 8 7 6 5 4 3 2 1

Printed in the U.S.A.

L.A. SECRET POLICE

Inside the LAPD Elite Spy Network

Mike Rothmiller
and
Ivan G. Goldman

POCKET BOOKS

New York   London   Toronto   Sydney   Tokyo   Singapore

Acknowledgments

To my family and friends.

Some of you know the role you played, but others do not. Simply put, you were there when I needed you the most. You are the people who mean everything in the world to me. You are the people who, by way of your love and support, saw me through the most difficult time in my life.

To Pat & Mayda McMillan, Frank & Michelle McManus, John Burrud, Marlene Burrud, Tim Lassig, Chuck & Marie Elfsten, Phyllis O'Connor, Matt & Pat Thomson, Dan & Pat O'Connor, Jon & Nan Rager, Frank & Carol Skrah, Michael Stone, Pete "Lima" Acuna, Steve & Debbie Underwood and Dr. Leonard Kram. And to the very special people who passed away before I completed this project. I'll never forget you: my dad, John Rothmiller; my father-in-law, Frank O'Connor; and my second dad, Bill Burrud.

And to the three women who have played the most important roles in my life: my wife, Nancy—I don't know where I'd be without you; to my mom, Betty Rothmiller—you have always been there; and to Mary Ann Healy, my attorney and a truly caring person.

And a special thanks to my new friends who have played an important role in this project: Michael Hamilburg, a great agent; Dana Isaacson and Judith Regan, terrific editors; and Ivan Goldman, a very talented writer.

I thank you all.

Mike Rothmiller

To my beloved family, and in memory of my beloved sister, Marilen Goldman Dolgin

Ivan Goldman

Authors' Note

There were instances when we decided that we had to report the unfounded rumors and unfortunate surveillance work of OCID. Truly, this was done sparingly, to prove a point with even greater force against such abuses. We particularly apologize to John Van De Kamp and Jerry Brown. The only way to show just how unjustified were the investigations into their private lives was to name them specifically, along with the foolish, malevolent probes undertaken against them.